Perspectives in Psychology

INTRODUCTORY PSYCHOLOGY

This new and rapidly expanding series of titles is aimed at A-level Psychology students in sixth forms and further education colleges and at those wishing to obtain an overview of psychology. The books are easy to use, with comprehensive notes written in coherent language; clear flagging of key concepts; relevant and interesting illustrations; well-defined objectives and further reading sections to each chapter; and self-assessment questions at regular intervals throughout the text.

Published

DEVELOPMENTAL PSYCHOLOGY: From Infancy to
 Adulthood
Ann Birch and Tony Malim

SOCIAL PSYCHOLOGY
Tony Malim and Ann Birch

PERSPECTIVES IN PSYCHOLOGY
Tony Malim, Ann Birch and Alison Wadeley

Series Standing Order

If you would like to receive future titles in this series as they are published, you can make use of our standing order facility. To place a standing order please contact your bookseller or, in case of difficulty, write to us at the address below with your name and address and the name of the series. Please state with which title you wish to begin your standing order. (If you live outside the United Kingdom we may not have the rights for your area, in which case we will forward your order to the publisher concerned.)

Customer Services Department, Macmillan Distribution Ltd, Houndmills, Basingstoke, Hampshire, RG21 2XS, England.

PERSPECTIVES IN PSYCHOLOGY

Tony Malim
Ann Birch
Alison Wadeley

MACMILLAN

First published 1992 by
THE MACMILLAN PRESS LTD
Houndmills, Basingstoke, Hampshire RG21 2XS
and London
Companies and representatives
throughout the world

ISBN 0–333–57420–6 hardcover
ISBN 0–333–56500–2 paperback

A catalogue record for this book is available
from the British Library.

Printed in Hong Kong

Reprinted 1992

Contents

3 Philosophical Issues in Psychology 47

4 Research Methods 103

5 What Do Psychologists Do? 133

6 Psychology and Scientific Method 159

List of Figures

Preface

This book aims to provide those engaged in the study of psychology with an overview of psychological science. It begins with an account of the historical background of psychology, looking at different strands within its development from being a branch of philosophy to its emergence as a science. Chapter 2 examines different theoretical approaches which have developed and which currently influence psychological theory and practice.

Chapter 3 presents a discussion of major issues and controversies in psychology, such as the nature–nurture debate, idiographic/nomothetic approaches, reductionism, free will and determinism, consciousness and so on. Research methods in psychology are described and discussed critically in Chapter 4, while Chapter 5 looks at vocational fields open to psychologists. Finally Chapter 6 critically discusses scientific method as it is employed in psychology, the use of animals in research and the question of ethics.

The authors have attempted to present this overview simply and concisely in the form of comprehensive notes. There is, of course, a thin dividing line between clarity and succinctness on the one hand and oversimplification and distortion on the other. Every effort has been made to avoid the latter. Psychology is a rich and varied discipline containing many complex ideas. Some of these cannot be adequately expressed briefly, therefore at the end of each chapter there are suggestions for appropriate further reading.

For the independent student each chapter begins with objectives to be met during the study of the chapter and each section within chapters ends with self-assessment questions, so that the reader may test his/her understanding of the section. The reader is advised to work through the text a section at a time and to consider the self-assessment questions as they present themselves and again after further reading has been undertaken.

The authors believe that this book will meet a long-felt need and that readers will find it both enjoyable and useful in relation to their study of psychology. It is a book which students may look at when new to psychology and again when they are more familiar with the subject.

Tony Malim
Ann Birch
Alison Wadeley

DARWIN'S THEORY LIVES ! I SURVIVED
THE MONDAY MORNING RUSH-HOUR !

Psychology : An Historical Sketch 1

At the end of this chapter you should be able to:

1. propose a definition of psychology;
2. trace the historical development of psychology from its philosophical roots to its emergence as a separate, scientific discipline;
3. reach an understanding of the concept of schools of psychology;
4. describe and make some assessment of the schools of structuralism, functionalism, behaviourism, Gestalt psychology and
   psychoanalysis; and
5. identify some of the contributions made by these schools to
   contemporary psychology.

SECTION I   EARLY BEGINNINGS

What Is Psychology?

Perhaps the most widely accepted definition of psychology is that it
is the scientific study of behaviour and experience. That is to say
that, through systematic research, psychologists aim to explore
questions about the way human beings, and sometimes animals,
behave and how they experience the world around them. This
apparently simple and straightforward definition requires further
explanation if the reader is to gain an adequate view of the nature

of psychology and, indeed, the whole of this book is concerned with that explanation. The aim of this chapter is to give a brief account of the early development of psychology and to examine significant events in the history of the subject up to about the middle of the twentieth century.

Psychology as a scientific discipline has a short history – only just over a hundred years. As a branch of philosophy it dates back to the time of Plato and Aristotle. The word 'psychology' is of Greek origin: 'psyche' can be freely translated as 'mind' or 'soul' and 'logos' indicates 'study' or 'line of teaching'; thus we have 'study of the mind'. This definition exemplifies what psychology was essentialy about up to the end of the nineteenth century.

It was in 1879 that Wilhelm Wundt opened the first psychological laboratory in Leipzig, Germany. It is generally agreed that this event heralded the beginning of psychology as a scientific discipline in its own right. Prior to this, psychology had generally been regarded as a branch of philosophy. Before we consider the development of psychology as a scientific discipline, it will be of benefit to examine briefly the influence of some philosophical ideas.

Pre-scientific Psychology

René Descartes (1596–1650), the French philosopher, had an important influence on the development of psychology as a discipline distinct from philosophy. Before Descartes, human beings tended to be viewed by philosophers as unique, mysterious products of God's will, whose mental life was beyond rational explanation. Influenced by scientific discoveries of the time in the field of medicine, most notably Harvey's discovery of the blood circulatory system, Descartes adopted a more analytical stance. He attempted to view the human being as a machine which could be studied and whose workings could be understood and explained. In his theory of **dualism** he made a distinction between the mind (thinking, remembering, knowing) and the body (physiological processes). The interaction of mind and body, he believed, took place in the brain and the seat of the mind was narrowed down to the pineal gland, a structure in the brain which serves to initiate hormonal activity.

The seventeenth century also saw the birth of the British

Empiricist Movement, led by a group of philosophers, the most notable of whom were John Locke and Thomas Hobbes. The empiricists attempted to make sense of the human mind through the use of systematic and objective methods of study, rather than through reasoning or intuition. Mental life, they contended, was composed of 'ideas' which arose from sensory experience and entered the mind by means of perception. In contrast to Descartes, who believed that some ideas are present at birth, the empiricists saw the development of the mind as arising from experiences of and interaction with the environment. Thus the early seeds of the nature–nurture debate were sown (see Chapter 3, Section III).

In the early part of the nineteenth century there was a strong upsurge of philosophical opinion which contended that the study of human mental activity was worthy of attention in its own right outside of the discipline of philosophy. This move was greatly advanced by the work of a group of German physiologists – Weber, who used weights to study muscle sense, Helmholz, who made an outstanding contribution to the study of vision and hearing, and Fechner, who investigated visual discrimination and perception. The findings of these early physiologists greatly influenced psychology as we know it today.

Scientific Psychology

As previously indicated, the establishment of psychology as a scientific discipline in its own right is generally linked to the setting up in 1879 of the first psychological laboratory by Wilhelm Wundt. Before looking further at the work of Wundt and his contemporaries, it might be useful to examine the concept of **schools** of **psychology.**

Schools of Psychology

As psychology developed as a discipline which was founded on the use of empirical methods (based on observation and the collection of data) there emerged a number of different schools of thought. Schools, in this context, can best be thought of as groups of psychologists who held common beliefs about both the subject matter of psychology, that is what facets of mental functioning should be studied, and what methods of study should be used. Most schools developed as a revolt against traditional methods and beliefs at the time. However they did not always replace earlier schools, but sometimes existed alongside them. Schools, as such, do not now exist, but each has provided ideas (some more influential than others) which have influenced contemporary approaches to psychology (see Chapter 2). Therefore a knowledge of them can help us to make sense of the multitude of ideas and methods which currently characterise psychology.

Sections II to V contain a brief description of six major schools of psychology: structuralism, functionalism, associationism, behaviourism, Gestalt psychology and psychoanalysis.

Self-assessment Questions

1. How would you define psychology?
2. What event is generally regarded as the beginning of psychology as a scientific discipline distinct from philosophy?
3. In what way did the philosopher, René Descartes, influence philosophical thinking about the nature of the human mind?
4. Outline the main contributions to psychology of
   (a) the British Empiricists;
   (b) the nineteenth-century physiologists, Weber, Helmholz and Fechner.
5. What do you understand by 'schools of psychology'?

SECTION II STRUCTURALISM AND FUNCTIONALISM

Structuralism

Inspired by the pioneering work of Fechner and other scientists, **Wilhelm Wundt** and his many collaborators founded the school of structuralism. Wundt believed that psychology should concern itself with the elementary processes of **conscious experience**. The structure of consciousness and immediate mental experience, he contended, could be broken down into basic elements and compounds in the same way that, in chemistry, one can describe the structure of water or air.

The elements of conscious experience were considered to be of two kinds:

- **sensations** – sights, sounds, tastes, smells and touch, which arise from stimulation of the sense organs; and
- **feelings** – love, fear, joy and so on.

The term **image** was also used to describe experiences not actually present,

Three primary questions were addressed:

1. What are the elements of experience?
2. How are they combined?
3. What causes the elements to combine?

An experience such as meeting and recognising an old friend in the street was thought to be composed of many independent sensations, feelings and images, which were drawn together and synthesised by the mind.

In an effort to study the elements of consciousness in what they believed was an analytical and objective way, structuralists devised a technique known as **introspection**. This simply means that people were asked to consider and report on their own mental processes as they experienced a particular object or event. This was to be done in a pre-specified and systematic way and required much training. For example, to be introspective about a flower, the reporter would be asked to describe the sensations of experiencing it in terms of its shape, size, colour, texture and so on.

The method of introspection proved difficult and inadequate, largely because of conflicting findings between introspectionists in different laboratories. Reaching agreement on the basic elements of a particular mental experience proved an impossible task and (predictably, perhaps) reporting on mental activity in humans was not quite so straightforward as observing what happens in a test-tube when two chemicals are combined.

Another prominent member of the structuralist school, Edward Titchener, developed and extended Wundt's ideas and later introduced them to the USA.

Structuralism declined in the early 1920s, partly through the failure of introspective methods to provide a coherent and generally accepted account of human mental activity and partly through the emergence of schools which offered alternative approaches to the study of psychology. These schools included functionalism, behaviourism and Gestalt psychology, each of which developed at least in part as a reaction against structuralism.

Functionalism

Whilst the structuralists emphasised the structure of mental activity, the functionalists were concerned with the purposes, or **functions**, of mental processes. Functionalism was strongly influenced by biology and many of the concepts 'borrowed' from that discipline continue to influence psychology today.

The work and ideas of **Charles Darwin** had a monumental impact on the emergence of functional psychology. Darwin's revolutionary theory of evolution provided an account of the way living organisms change and develop over time through a process of **natural selection**. Living organisms have characteristics such as extreme strength, speed of movement and temperament, which are variable even within the same species. Organisms whose characteristics were best suited to their environment survived and reproduced, while organisms whose characteristics were less adaptable died out. Survivors would transmit to the next generation those characteristics which enabled them to survive. In this way a particular species might change quite extensively over several generations and, in some cases, an entirely new species could evolve.

The notion that humans had descended from animals was revolutionary – and shocking to many people. Amongst psychologists it led to a belief, which for many still persists, that by studying animals a greater understanding might be reached about the nature of human beings. (See Chapter 6, Section II for a discussion of the use of animals in psychological research.) Darwin's work also drew attention to the importance of studying individual differences between members of a species. This idea was taken up and continues to provide an importance focus in psychology today, particularly in the field of psychometrics (see Chapter 4, Section V).

William James (1842–1910) was a leading figure in functional psychology and his work has made a very significant impact on contemporary psychology. Influenced greatly by Darwin, James held that the function of consciousness was to enable humans to behave in ways which would aid survival through adaptation to the environment. Where these adaptive behaviours were repeated frequently they became **habits**. Habits, James believed, provided stability and predictability in society.

The range of topics studied by James was immense and few psychologists would disagree that he was responsible for opening up the scope of psychology. In addition to a study of the functions of consciousness (see Chapter 3, Section V) and the role of habits, he turned his attention to emotions (see Chapter 3, Section VII) and to the concept of self. As with the structuralists, his main method of study was introspection, though he encouraged the use of experimentation. His emphasis on the importance of observing similarities and differences between varying species greatly influenced the development of comparative psychology. The work of John Dewey (1859–1952) at the University of Chicago further established the ideas of functionalism. This work led to a new trend, that of attempting to apply research findings to practical problems. For example, the first intelligence tests for use with children were developed by the functionalists.

Self-assessment Questions

1. What did the structuralists, led by Wundt, consider to be the appropriate subject matter of psychology?
2. Evaluate the use of introspection as an effective method of study.
3. How did the work of Charles Darwin influence or change the study of psychology?
4. What were the aims of the functionalists?
5. Outline some important contributions to contemporary psychology made by William James.

SECTION III ASSOCIATIONISM AND BEHAVIOURISM

Associationism

This refers to the movement concerned with studying the formation of associations in learning. The work of three scientists is important in this context: Herman Ebbinghaus (1850–1909), Edward Thorndike (1874–1949) and Ivan Pavlov (1849–1936). There follows a brief account of some of their main contributions.

The work of **Ebbinghaus** is often regarded as the basis of modern research into memory. Using himself as a subject and 'nonsense syllables' such as TAF, ZUC, POV as his experimental material, Ebbinghaus systematically studied factors which influence learning and forgetting. Nonsense syllables were used in preference to real words because Ebbinghaus believed they contained no meaning and thus offered a device which would enable him to study 'new' learning. New learning was regarded as the forming of associations within material which is not already associated with previous learning. His meticulous and painstaking methods of study, carried out over several years, produced much reliable quantified data. His work provided insights into remembering and forgetting which still hold good today. For example, he demonstrated that material is forgotten quite quickly in the first few hours after learning, but then the rate of forgetting becomes progressively slower.

Pavlov, a Russian physiologist, made a significant contribution to the study of learning through experiments with animals. During his investigations into the salivary reflex in dogs, Pavlov discovered that a stimulus, for example food (the unconditional stimulus), which is naturally linked with a particular reflex response, for example salivation (the unconditional response), can become associated with other stimuli which are present at the same time. In one series of experiments he showed that a dog, when offered food as a buzzer (the conditional stimulus) is sounded, will, after several presentations, begin to salivate when the buzzer alone is sounded. (Salivation now becomes the conditional response.) Thus an association is formed between the food and the buzzer and between the buzzer and the salivation response. This learning process became known as classical, or Pavlovian, conditioning. Its principles have since been applied to the study of human behaviour, for example as an explanation for the development of irrational fears or phobias.

Like Pavlov, **Thorndike** studied learning in animals. However, where Pavlov was interested in reflex, or *involuntary*, behaviour, Thorndike studied the associations formed between a stimulus and *voluntary* responses. His early experiments involved the use of a cat in a 'puzzle box' – a cage from which the animal could learn to escape by pulling a loop of string. Thorndike measured the time taken by the cat to escape as an indicator of learning. His data showed that learning the correct 'escape' behaviour happened gradually. The 'reward' (freedom), he contended, was responsible for 'stamping in' the appropriate response. This insight formed the basis of Thorndike's **Law of Effect**, which has been developed further by Skinner in his study of operant conditioning (see Chapter 2, Section III).

Behaviourism

While functionalism was at its height in the USA, a young student, **John Watson (1878–1958)** graduated in psychology at the University of Chicago. He went on to revolutionise psychology by changing it from the study of conscious experience to the study of behaviour. In an influential paper, 'Psychology as the behaviourist views it', in 1913, Watson attacked the structuralist emphasis on consciousness and mental experience and also condemned the use of introspection as a method which claimed to be reliable and objective. Psychology, he believed, should be about the study of observable behaviour that all could agree upon and the aim of psychology should be to describe, predict, understand and control behaviour. He contended that psychologists should '. . . never use the terms consciousness, mental states, introspectively verify, imagery and the like' (1913, p. 166).

Behaviourists did not reject the existence of mind and consciousness as critics have sometimes suggested. Rather they viewed these concepts as impossible to observe and contributing little to a scientific approach in psychology.

Watson and his colleagues believed that behaviour is moulded by experience. He therefore had a natural interest in learning and his view of learning relied to a great extent on Pavlov's account of classical conditioning described earlier. However complex a piece of behaviour might be, it was possible, behaviourists believed, to break it down and analyse it in basic **stimulus–response units**. Much of the behaviourists' research into learning was carried out on animals, rather than humans, partly because animals were easy to obtain and greater control could be exercised over their environments, and partly because they accepted the idea that humans and animals are related both physiologically and behaviourally.

Though Watson's view of the nature of human beings was considered by critics to be mechanistic and oversimplified, his focus on the study of observable behaviour allowed him to formulate clear hypotheses which could be tested by experimentation. This shift in emphasis towards the use of more objective and systematic methods was one of his greatest contributions to psychology.

Following the work of Watson and his followers, behaviourism gathered strength and its principles and methods of study became an integral part of psychology. By the middle of the twentieth century it was widely accepted that psychology was about the study of behaviour rather than conscious experience. This momentum has been sustained to a large extent in contemporary psychology by the efforts of the behaviourist, B.F. Skinner (see Chapter 2, Section III). Skinner extended principles derived from his work with animals to a consideration of human behaviour. However, as will become clear in Chapter 2, although behaviourism has left an indelible mark on contemporary psychology, alternative perspectives have been offered, largely through the emergence of cognitive psychology (Section IV) and humanistic psychology (Section V), which have modified its influence and endorsed the value of also studying mental processes and conscious experience.

Self-assessment Questions

1. Briefly outline the main contributions made by the associationists.
2. Outline Watson's objections to structuralist psychology.
3. What did the behaviourists consider should be the aims of psychology?
4. Briefly explain the process of learning known as classical conditioning.
5. Why was Watson particularly concerned with the study of learning?
6. In what way did the behaviourists influence methods of study in psychology?

SECTION IV   GESTALT PSYCHOLOGY

Functionalism and behaviourism came into being in the USA partly as a protest against structuralism. Around the same time, another movement against structuralism developed in Germany – the Gestalt School. The leading proponents of the Gestalt view were Max Wertheimer (1880–1943), Kurt Koffka (1876–1941) and Wolfgang Köhler (1887–1967).

Gestalt psychologists opposed the atomist approach of the structuralists and later the behaviourists. **Atomism** is a belief that, to understand a phenomenon, it is best to break it down and investigate its constituent parts. (See Chapter 3 for a discussion of the related concept of reductionism.) In contrast, Gestalt psychologists argued that people perceive the world in 'wholes'. 'The whole is greater than the sum of its parts' exemplifies this view. Gestalt, roughly translated, means 'whole', 'shape' or 'configuration'.

Wertheimer produced an early demonstration of this holistic approach through his experiments on **apparent movement**. He showed that, when two lights were presented a small distance apart and then switched on and off alternately, at certain time intervals a person reported seeing not two lights being lit, but one light which appeared to move from one location to the other. Wertheimer called this effect the **phi phenomenon**. He claimed that it contradicted the structuralist view that perception could be understood by analysing the basic elements of the perceiver's experience. The phi phenomenon is more familiar to us in the form of apparent movement in illuminated advertisements and the like. Further research by the Gestaltists led to the development of a set of principles of perceptual organisation. Such organisation, they believed, arose through the brain's innate ability to structure and organise the perceptual field into meaningful 'patterns' rather than perceiving the separate elements. Figure 1.1 illustrates some of the main Gestalt principles of organisation: figure/ground; proximity; similarity; closure.

The Gestalt principles of organisation can be subsumed under the overall guiding principle of **Prägnanz**. This refers to the principle governing the brain's attempt to perceive objects in the 'best' and most meaningful way. Critics have pointed out that these principles are purely descriptive and offer no explanations as

FIGURE 1.1
Gestalt Principles of Perceptual Organisation

Figure/ground: focusing attention on an object causes it to 'stand out' sharply from its context, whilst the context or 'ground' is less clear. This ambiguous figure illustrates a situation where the figure and ground reverses as the brain switches attention from one to the other.

Proximity: the dots are perceived in groups of two rather than as eight separate items.

Similarity: these equally spaced dots are perceived in groups of two.

Closure: this figure is perceived as a circle rather than as four curved lines.

to how or why the brain operates in this way.

Learning and problem solving also received much attention from the Gestaltists. **Köhler** investigated problem solving in apes. One study involved an animal in a cage with food out of reach beyond the cage. Inside the cage were a number of sticks which, if slotted together, were long enough to reach the food. After a period of inactivity, the animal quite suddenly solved the problem by slotting the sticks together and reaching for the food. Kohler claimed that, because all the elements for the solutions were available, the animal perceived the problem situation as a whole, formed a hypothesis about its solution and responded appropriately. He called this process 'insightful learning'.

The tendency of the Gestalt psychologists to rely for their data on subjective observations and reports of conscious experience, rather than carefully controlled behavioural methods, attracted criticism from the behaviourists. Gestaltists have also been accused of posing more problems than they actually solved. Nonetheless the influence of Gestalt psychology is great in some areas of contemporary psychology, for example in the study of perception and problem solving. Also the concept of 'wholeness' has been adopted in Gestalt approaches to therapy. Gestalt views can also be detected in some contemporary approaches to learning in the field of education. For example, work on discovery learning is rooted in early Gestalt ideas.

Self-assessment Questions

1. How might the term 'atomism' be applied to the work of the structuralists and the behaviourists?
2. Explain how the views of the Gestalt psychologists contrasted with the atomist approach of the structuralists and behaviourists.
3. How does the phi phenomenon illustrate the views held by the Gestaltists about perception?
4. What, according to the Gestaltists, is the purpose of perceptual organisation? Explain the principle of Prägnanz.
5. Briefly evaluate the contribution made to psychology by the Gestaltists.

SECTION V   PSYCHOANALYSIS

The school of psychoanalysis stands apart from the other schools in that the focus of attention is neither the nature or functions of consciousness, nor the stimulus–response links which influence behaviour. Psychoanalysis, which developed from the work and theories of Sigmund Freud (1856–1939), proposed an account of human mental activity which relied heavily on the notion of an **unconscious mind**.

Towards the end of the nineteenth century, science had been making huge advances and psychologists believed that the time was near when a full understanding of human mental life and behaviour would be reached. This view was shared by Freud, a young physician working as a neurologist in Vienna.

However, in the course of treating psychiatric patients over many years, Freud became convinced that many of the nervous symptoms displayed by patients could not be explained purely from a physiological point of view. Nor could the rational and systematic laws of science be applied to irrational and self-defeating behaviours such as phobias (excessive fears) and conversion hysterias (physical complaints that have no apparent physiological cause). It was against this background that Freud developed his now famous psychoanalytic treatment of neurotic disorders. His therapeutic work led to the development of a comprehensive theory of personality and child development which focused largely on the emotional aspects of human functioning. Thus the term **psychoanalysis** can relate both to the treatment and to the theory. Freud's starting-point was a thorough analysis of his own personal experiences and the development of case studies of his patients.

Perhaps the best known case studies are those of Anna O and Little Hans. Below is a summary of some of the most significant aspects of Freud's theory:

1. The human personality contains and is greatly influenced by an unconscious mind harbouring repressed ('forgotten') memories which determine conscious thoughts and behaviour. A third level of consciousness, the pre-conscious, contains thoughts which may not be conscious at a given time, but which are accessible to us.

2. Human beings are born with a number of **instinctual drives** which regulate and motivate behaviour even in childhood. The source of these drives is **psychic energy** and the most powerful, the **libido**, is sexual in nature.

3. Experiences gained in early childhood have a crucially important influence on emotional and personality development.

4. The personality consists of three major structures: the **id**, which is biologically determined and represents all the instinctual drives which are inherited; the **ego**, which develops in order to help satisfy the id's needs in a socially acceptable way and the **superego**, representing the individual's internal framework (conscience and ego ideal) of the moral values which exist in the surrounding culture. Figure 1.2 illustrates the way in which these structures occupy different levels of consciousness in the mind: the conscious, the pre-conscious and the unconscious.

FIGURE 1.2
Structure of the Personality (Freud)

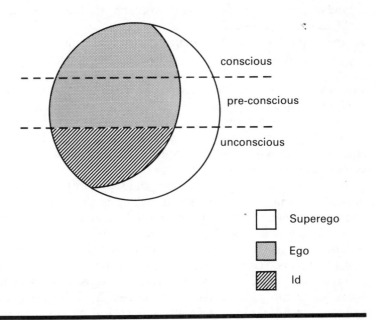

Freud's work attracted many followers, but his theory also generated much debate and controversy. His notion of 'infantile sexuality' outraged Victorian society. Many psychologists believed his methods of study to be unscientific and the concepts he employed vague and difficult to verify. Even among his original followers there were dissenters, such as **Carl Jung** and **Alfred Adler**, who eventually broke away from Freud to develop their own modified versions of his theory.

Jung's version of psychoanalytic theory differed from Freud's in two main respects:

1. Freud's conceptualisation of the unconscious mind was extended by Jung, who proposed that there existed also a **collective unconscious**. Jung reasoned that the human mind should contain a record of human experience in the same way as the body reveals the past structures of our ancestors. The collective unconscious, Jung believed, is not directly available to us but is revealed in the myths and artistic symbols that different cultures create. The collective unconscious contains archetypes, universal symbols that occur again and again in art, literature and religion.
2. The **libido** was seen by Jung as primarily spiritual in nature rather than essentially sexual, as had been posited by Freud.

Jung was also concerned with personality 'types'. He was responsible for proposing that humans are born with a temperament which is either **introverted** (primarily concerned with oneself) or **extraverted** (primarily concerned with the outside world). Introversion and extraversion have subsequently become important concepts in contemporary theories of personality.

Adler regarded the need for power and superiority as the most important human drive. Whilst not denying the existence of unconscious motives, he saw human motivation as being largely conscious. He had considerable success in treating mental disorders, particularly with young people suffering from minor maladjustments. His methods were quicker and simpler than those of Freud and therefore were less likely to become a dominating force in the life of a patient. Birth order, the order in which children are born within a family, was viewed by Adler as an important influence on the development of personality.

Psychoanalytic theory and methods of treating mental disorders are still a significant force in contemporary psychology. Many of Freud's original ideas have been adopted and in some cases modified by subsequent psychoanalytic theorists, known as post-Freudians (see Chapter 2, Section II).

Self-assessment Questions

1. Explain the two applications of the term 'psychoanalysis'.
2. What methods were used by Freud to arrive at his theory of personality and child development?
3. Briefly explain the Freudian concepts of unconscious mind and libido.
4. Outline the three structures of the personality proposed by Freud.
5. For what reasons did Freud's work attract criticism?
6. Briefly explain how the psychoanalytic theories of Jung and Adler differed from that of Freud.

FURTHER READING

E. Heidbreder, *Seven Psychologies* (Englewood Cliffs, NJ: Prentice-Hall, 1963).

K. Raaheim and J. Radford, *Your Introduction to Psychology* (Oslo: J.W. Cappelens Forlag a.s.; London: Sigma, 1984).

D. Schulz, *A History of Modern Psychology*, 4th edn (New York: Academic Press, 1987).

R.S. Woodworth and M.R. Sheehan, *Contemporary Schools of Psychology* (London: Methuen, 1965).

O.K. — SO WE'LL LEAVE THE FREE
ASSOCIATION AND GO INTO DREAM
ANALYSIS.

Theoretical Approaches to Psychology 2

At the end of this chapter you should be able to:

1. describe five major theoretical approaches to psychology: physiological, psychoanalytic, behaviourist, cognitive and humanistic;
2. discuss critically the strengths and limitations of each approach; and
3. discuss the use of different levels of explanation for psychological functioning.

INTRODUCTION

As outlined in Chapter 1, for the first 50 years or so of its existence as a separate discipline, psychology was organised around separate schools, each with its own distinct ideas of what psychology should be about and how it should be studied. Psychologists tended to identify themselves as structuralists, functionalists, behaviourists, psychoanalysts or Gestaltists. Today, with the realisation that the problems psychologists have set themselves will not be solved by one particular set of ideas and methods, it is accepted that many different routes must be taken if a full understanding is to be reached about psychological functioning. Psychologists are now often classified according to their professional commitments – clinical psychologist or educational psychologist, for example – or to their specific fields of study, such as social, developmental or cognitive psychology (see Chapter 5).

However, though schools as such no longer exist, within each field of psychology can be seen many different **approaches** to the study of psychological phenomena, and some of the ideas of the early schools continue to influence many of the modern-day approaches. 'Approach', in this context is not easy to define exactly, but it is to do with basic assumptions that are made about what human beings are like, theories used in order to help explain human and animal behaviour and the kinds of research methods used to study them. For example, the learning theory approach, influenced heavily by the behaviourist school, still strongly emphasises the effects of the environment on psychological functioning and continues to use the concept of reinforcement in attempts to explain and change human behaviour. Also the experimental method is still the major technique used in research, in preference to more subjective methods.

Five major approaches in psychology are **physiological**, **psychoanalytic**, **behaviourist** (or learning theory), **cognitive** and **humanistic**. Each will be discussed below. There is some overlap between these approaches and they should not be seen as separate, competing bodies of knowledge and theory. Rather they represent different but complementary views and methods of understanding psychological functioning.

SECTION I   THE PHYSIOLOGICAL APPROACH

Psychologists who take a physiological approach, as the name implies, look to biology as a means of describing and explaining psychological functioning. Our behaviour, even what we think and feel, is assumed to be linked to our physiological make-up. For example, schizophrenia may be seen as arising almost entirely from malfunctions in biochemical processes in the brain. Some of the labels attached to researchers who take this approach, albeit in rather different ways, are biopsychologist, neuropsychologist, psychobiologist and physiological psychologist.

Physiological psychologists are interested in a wide range of phenomena and issues. Research has developed rapidly over recent years into the functions of the nervous system (particularly the brain) and the hormonal system, and into how these two systems interact and influence behaviour and mental activity. Some of the questions that have been asked by scientists in the course of this research are: What activities occur in the nerve cells (neurons) of the brain and senses when we perceive patterns or colour? To what extent does the brain function as a single unit and to what extent as a collection of 'parts', each with its own particular function (localisation of brain functions)? What activities occur in the brain during different states of consciousness, such as wakefulness, sleep and coma? What are the links between the hormonal system and emotion, aggression and sex differences in behaviour? What physiological mechanisms underlie needs and motivations? What changes take place in the nervous system when a memory has been established or something has been learned?

Another aspect of the biological approach is interest in the role of heredity in behaviour. In the relatively short time since Darwin suggested that variations among individuals of a species could be passed on to future generations, much knowledge has accumulated regarding genetic transmission. For example, it is known that inheritance occurs through a chemical code carried in the genes. However, while the transmission of physical characteristics is well understood, the role of heredity in behavioural characteristics such as intelligence and personality is less clear-cut. Linked to this is interest in the relative importance of heredity and environment in the development of psychological characteristics – **the nature–nurture** debate, a long-standing controversy in psychology (see Chapter 3, Section III).

Reductionism and the Mind/Body Problem

There are some scientists who believe that all psychological phenomena can be explained by reference to ('reduced to') physiological activity, particularly brain processes. This philosophical viewpoint has been termed **reductionism**. The term may be used also in relation to views held by behavioural and other psychologists.

Reductionism in relation to physiological psychology implies that, if we are to understand psychological functioning, we must analyse these functions in terms of ever smaller units of analysis, such as nerve activity, muscle movements or chemical processes.

This view, taken to its logical conclusions, could lead to psychological explanations of behaviour becoming redundant. (For a more detailed discussion of reductionism, see Chapter 3, Section I.)

The reductionist issue is closely linked to a continuing and extremely controversial issue, that of the **mind/body problem**. This issue is concerned with the relationship between the mind (or awareness) and the neurophysiological processes within the body, how the two interact and the influence of one on the other. The debate began in the seventeenth century, with the work of the philosopher, **René Descartes** (see Chapter 1). (Descartes' theory (known as dualism) put forward the view that the human body, like that of animals, was basically a machine. However what distinguished humans from animals was the existence in the former of a soul which was intangible but which interacted with the physical body through the pineal gland located in the brain.

In modern times most people would equate the term 'mind' with 'brain'. But the word 'mind' was originally created to identify a psychological rather than a physiological concept. The mind is usually regarded as the root of awareness, or consciousness, rather than as a physiological mechanism. Many examples exist of the effect of body on mind (a cup of coffee may act as a stimulant) and also of mind on body (for some the prospect of flying or even a visit to the dentist can produce trembling and sweating). Also research has confirmed that the brain is involved in the experience of consciousness, though it is not certain how and to what extent. Therefore the question remains: if it is impossible to link the intangible mind to a particular part of the body, how can we study the interaction between the two? There is currently no adequate answer. However knowledge is constantly expanding and, as our understanding of physiological mechanisms increases, it becomes clear that mind and body are closely integrated.

Some Research Findings from Physiological Psychology

There follows a brief outline of some research which has focused on the physiological mechanisms underlying behaviour. The aim here is to provide the reader with a 'feel' for the kinds of investigations carried out and some of the techniques used.

1. In 1861, **Paul Broca**, a doctor, demonstrated by **post-mortem**

autopsy that a patient's inability to speak arose from a defect in a specific area of the brain. This evidence of **localisation of brain function** contributes to the gradually emerging view that behaviour had a physical base.

2. In the 1920s, **Karl Lashley** carried out a series of classic experiments in which he demonstrated that learning and memory in rats is impaired if part of the cortex of the brain is removed. Lashley used a technique known as **ablation**, the removal of parts of the brain by surgery or by burning out with electrodes. Many of his experiments demonstrated that the amount of brain tissue destroyed appeared to be more important to the animal's behaviour than the specific part of the brain involved (Lashley, 1929). He believed that all parts of the brain were probably involved in every action (the Law of Mass Action).

3. Much research has been carried out into **electrical stimulation of the brain (ESB)**. ESB involves the stimulation of neurons by means of a mild electrical current passed through an implanted electrode. Typically the main aim of this research is to investigate the effects of such stimulation on behaviour, particularly emotions. In the 1950s, using ESB, **Olds and Milner** identified **pleasure centres** in the brains of rats – areas which, when stimulated, led the rat to return to the area of the cage where it had been stimulated.

4. Much well-established research has highlighted the close interaction between mental processes and physiological changes within the body. **Hans Selye (1956, 1974)** has pioneered research into the physiological changes associated with stress in both animals and humans. Selye's work led him to propose the **General Adaptation Syndrome** (GAS), which describes the hormonal, biochemical and other bodily changes which occur and which interact with psychological factors within the individual during the experience of stress.

5. A great deal of research has been carried out in an attempt to understand the nature and causes of **schizophrenia**. Some of this work has indicated the influence of social, cultural and family factors on the development of the condition. A major line of enquiry has focused on possible biological differences between schizophrenic individuals and other people. For example, evidence is accumulating that schizophrenia, or some

variants of it, may have a genetic base. Using advanced techniques of molecular biology, Sherrington *et al.* (1988) have located a genetic abnormality in members of a family having an unusually high incidence of schizophrenia. Research such as this does not, however, rule out other possible causes of schizophrenia.

Evaluation of the Physiological Approach

The physiological approach endeavours to work towards an understanding and explanation of the biological basis of behaviour. It is unique as an approach within psychology in the range of factors it considers and in the level at which it seeks to explain them. The physiological approach is the only one which attempts to relate behaviour to the workings and genetic make-up of the body. Other approaches, for example psychoanalysis, may subscribe to the view that behaviour is biologically based, but the concepts used and the phenomena studied are largely psychological rather than physiological.

As already noted, much valuable evidence has accumulated about the biological basis of behaviour. However physiological psychology is not yet sufficiently advanced to offer total explanations for memory, stress, learning, emotions and so on. Moreover the complexity of the physiological system and the countless environmental influences that may affect it make it difficult to predict behaviour and explain it in purely physiological terms. This complexity and the way in which factors interact make it difficult also to draw specific conclusions about one factor, for example genetic links with schizophrenia, without taking into account other factors, such as cultural or family influences.

Some psychologists are afraid that overemphasising physiological links with behaviour may lead to reductionist explanations (see Chapter 3, Section I) which override the value of psychological explanations. A more positive view would be to accept that physiological mechanisms underlie behaviour and should be studied. Insights from this research may be used to complement purely psychological observations and measurements, resulting in a more complete description and explanation of behaviour. (Further examples of physiological psychology can be found in

Chapter 3 in the sections on reductionism, consciousness, motivation and emotion and in Chapter 5, Section I.)

Self-assessment Questions

1. Briefly outline some of the issues which concern physiological psychologists.
2. What do you understand by the mind/body problem?
3. Briefly describe two pieces of research carried out by physiological psychologists.
4. What are the strengths and limitations of the physiological approach?

SECTION II THE PSYCHOANALYTIC APPROACH

The psychoanalytic approach arises from Freud's theory of the **unconscious mind**. As previously noted, the term **psychoanalysis** may refer either to a form of therapy or to a theory of the human mind and behaviour. A brief outline of some of the central concepts of Freud's psychoanalytic theory has already been given in Chapter 1, Section V.

Psychoanalysis as a Therapy

Psychoanalysis as a therapy is very widely used in the treatment of neuroses and sometimes in the treatment of non-neurotic disorders. There is an assumption by psychoanalysts that it is in the unconscious part of the personality that conflict occurs. Therefore the aim of psychoanalysis is to explore the individual's unconscious mind in order to understand the dynamic of abnormal behaviour. During treatment the individual is encouraged to re-experience traumatic events and feelings encountered in childhood, express them in a safe context and then return them, devoid of anxiety, to the unconscious.

In classical psychoanalysis, therapy involves **transference** – the client's projection and displacement of thoughts and feelings onto the analyst; **free association**, where the client says whatever comes into his/her mind, no matter how trivial or irrelevant it may seem;

and **dream analysis**, which involves the analyst interpreting the content of the client's dreams.

Though the psychoanalytic process may sound quite straightforward, it is usually difficult and time-consuming.

Post-Freudians

Many of Freud's original ideas have been adapted and modified by subsequent psychoanalytic theorists, known as post-Freudians. Much of their work, a selection of which is outlined below, has been centrally concerned with clinical problems and the treatment of mental disorders.

Anna Freud, Sigmund Freud's daughter, was part of the Continental school of psychoanalysis, though she came to Britain shortly before the Second World War, at the same time as her father. As part of the movement, starting in the 1930s, to apply a full psychoanalytic approach to problems of childhood, Anna Freud worked largely with older children and adolescents.

The publication of *The Ego and the Mechanisms of Defence* (1936) encouraged a new tendency in psychoanalysis to attach more importance to the conscious mind, or ego, than had previously been the case. Anna Freud believed that the term 'psychoanalysis' could not be applied to any technique which focused attention on the unconscious mind to the exclusion of everything else. She also expressed the belief that her father had overstressed the influence of sexuality in early childhood and had neglected its importance in adolescence. She saw adolescence as a time when there is an upsurge in the activity of the libido (sexual energy) and young people experience renewed sexual feelings and strivings. The intensity of these inner drives, she contended, results in excessive emotional upset as the adolescent tries to cope with the resulting impulses and desires.

Melanie Klein was one of the leading figures in European psychoanalysis but, like Anna Freud, established herself in Britain in the 1930s. From her background as a nursery teacher she related much of Freud's psychoanalytic theory to the development of very young children. She developed a therapeutic technique for analysing children's play which made it possible for psychoanalytic principles to be applied to children as young as two to six years old. **Play therapy** is the term used to describe a means through which a psychoanalyst can use play to get in touch with a child's unconscious in order to help him/her deal with emotional difficulties.

In Klein's version of play therapy, simple play materials were used, for example male and female dolls, small models of familiar objects, such as cars, wheelbarrows or swings, and materials such as paper, string, clay and water. The child was allowed free access to play with all these objects and materials while the analyst knelt and attended to the content of the play. Occasionally she would offer an interpretation of the play to the child and would encourage **transference**; that is, she encouraged the child to transfer feelings towards the parents onto herself. Interpretations of the phantasy life of the child as revealed in play were given. Klein's methods offered new insights into development during the earliest years of childhood. Her views and methods dominated the mainstream of orthodox psychoanalysis in Britain. Prominent analysts such as D.W. Winnicott and John Bowlby, who were closely associated with the Tavistock Clinic where Klein worked, supported and were influenced by her views.

Erik Erikson began his psychoanalytic training with Anna Freud, whose interest in child analysis greatly influenced his work. In 1933, Erikson left Europe and began to practise as a child analyst in the USA. Though subscribing to much orthodox psychoanalytic theory, Erikson believed that Freud overemphasised the role of sexuality in the personality and neglected the importance of the social forces which influence development. He therefore proposed a series of **psychosocial stages** (rather than psychosexual stages, as proposed by Freud) through which an individual passes during his/her lifetime. In contrast to Freud, who particularly emphasised the importance of the childhood years for later personality, Erikson viewed the stages of development as covering the whole lifespan. Each stage was marked by a central crisis, the successful management of which would lead to the development and maintenance of a well-balanced personality.

Much of Erikson's clinical practice was carried out with troubled adolescents. His view that the conflict of 'identity versus role confusion' encountered during adolescence, is the central crisis of all development, has received wide support amongst psychologists. Erikson has made a substantial contribution to the field of developmental psychology and in particular to the area of lifespan development where his theory is the single most important influence.

Evaluation of the Psychoanalytic Approach

The psychoanalytic approach attracts both wide acclaim and vigorous criticism. Freud's theory has made a monumental contribution to our understanding of the human personality. His emphasis on the importance of early childhood for later personality development and his attempt to account for individual differences in development have stimulated a great deal of research. His theory has also offered insights which have greatly influenced disciplines such as art, English literature and history. As already noted, psychoanalytic methods of treating mental disorders are widely used by many psychologists. Criticisms of the psychoanalytic approach can be summarised as follows:

1. Though there is an abundance of research which claims to offer supporting evidence for psychoanalytic theory (for example, Kline, 1984), alternative explanations are often available to account for the findings. Eysenck and Wilson (1973) claim: (a) that, because many of the processes described by Freud, for example instinctual drives and defence mechanisms, cannot be directly observed, the generation of precise and testable hypotheses is difficult; and (b) that Freud's use of the clinical case study method, unsupported by quantitative data or statistical analyses, renders his theory vague and difficult to verify. Also his study of a limited sample of adults makes it difficult to generalise his theory to all human beings.
2. Attention has been drawn to the problems encountered in trying to assess the effectiveness of psychoanalysis as a therapy, largely arising from the controversy over what constitutes a 'cure'. Eysenck (1952) reviewed five studies of the effectiveness of psychoanalysis and concluded that it achieved little that would not have occurred without therapy. However, using different criteria of the notion of 'cure', Bergin (1971) put the success rate of psychoanalysis at 83 per cent.

(See Chapter 3, Section II for an account of where the psychoanalytic approach stands on the issue of free will and determinism. See also Chapter 6, Section I for a discussion of psychoanalysis in relation to the scientific method.)

Self-assessment Questions

1. What is the main aim of psychoanalysis as a therapy?
2. Give an outline of the views or work of one of the post-Freudians.
3. What are the main strengths and shortcomings of the psychoanalytic approach?

SECTION III THE BEHAVIOURIST (OR LEARNING THEORY) APPROACH

Where physiological psychologists focus on genetics and an individual's biological make-up, behaviourists or learning theorists focus on the influence of the environment. They choose not to be concerned with the internal mechanisms which occur inside the organism. Questions likely to be explored are: Under what conditions might certain behaviour occur? What might be the effects of various stimuli on behaviour? How do the consequences of behaviour affect that behaviour? Questions such as these are relevant to the behaviourist view that human beings are **shaped** through constant interactions with the environment. Put more simply, learning and experience determine the kind of person you become.

The behaviourist approach to psychological functioning is rooted in the work of associationists, Ivan Pavlov and Edward Thorndike, and the early behaviourists, John Watson and Clark Hull, all of whom studied learning in the form of conditioning (see Chapter 1, Section III). Pavlov studied the conditioning of reflex responses, or **classical conditioning**, whilst Thorndike's work focused on the conditioning of voluntary behaviour, now referred to as **operant conditioning**, and later researched further by B.F. Skinner.

Behaviourism had a profound influence on the course of psychology during the first half of the twentieth century. Its offshoot, **stimulus–response psychology**, is still influential today. Stimulus–response psychology, which is epitomised by the work of the modern-day behaviourist, B.F. Skinner, in operant condition-ing, studies the stimuli which elicit behavioural responses, the rewards and punishments that influence these responses and the changes in behaviour brought about by manipulating patterns of rewards and punishments. This approach does not concern itself with the mental processes which occur between the stimulus and the response.

Skinner, in his *Behaviour of Organisms* (1938), described ex-periments he conducted with rats and later with pigeons. For instance, he conditioned rats to press a bar in a 'Skinner box' in return for a reward of food. He was able to measure learning accurately under closely controlled conditions, varying the fre-quency of reward, or **reinforcement**, and sometimes applying irrelevant stimuli. Though he started his research with animals, Skinner worked towards a theory of conditioning which could include humans. This work is described in *Science and Human Behaviour* (1953).

Some Practical Applications of the Behaviourist Approach

The influence of the behaviourist approach, with its emphasis on the manipulation of behaviour through patterns of reinforcement and punishment, can be seen in many practical situations, both in education and in psychotherapy. Below is a brief account of some of these practical applications.

Programmed Learning

Skinner applied the principles of operant conditioning to the formal learning situation. He developed a system known as 'programmed learning', in which teaching machines are sometimes used, although it can take the form of written self-teaching units. The material to be learned is broken down into a large number of small segments, or **frames**. The student works through the frames sequentially and is required to respond at the end of each one. Correct responses receive reinforcement in the form of **immediate feedback** and, if correct, the learner proceeds to the next frame. In this way behaviour is shaped. The sequence described above is known as a linear programme. A more complex sequence, known as a branching programme, can also be used.

Programmed learning was not adopted as widely as had been

envisaged by Skinner. Reports of its effectiveness relative to conventional learning methods are variable.

Behavioural Therapies

Therapeutic techniques based on conditioning processes are usually referred to as either **behaviour modification** or **behaviour therapy**. Walker (1984) has proposed that techniques based on operant conditioning should be referred to as behaviour modification and that techniques which rely upon the principles of classical conditioning should be known as behaviour therapy. This distinction is used in the descriptions which follow.

Behaviour modification This is a technique which is used to change or remove unwanted behaviour. Its central principle, taken from operant conditioning, is that behaviour which has favourable consequences, that is, which is **positively reinforced**, is likely to be repeated and behaviour which is ignored is likely to die out. The desired behaviour is broken down into a sequence of small steps. Each step achieved is immediately rewarded, but gradually more and more of the required behaviour is demanded before the reward is given. This process is known as **behaviour shaping** through successive approximations.

Behaviour modification has been widely used in clinical settings with mentally handicapped children and adults and especially with autistic children. Typically a shaping technique is used. For instance, Lovaas (1973) developed a programme to modify the behaviour of autistic children from withdrawal to talking and social interaction. Appropriate responses were initially rewarded with sweets. Later, when the children became more responsive, cuddling was used as a reinforcement for 'good' behaviour.

Token economy systems are based on the principle of **secondary** reinforcement. Tokens are given in exchange for desirable or acceptable behaviours. These can then be exchanged for **primary** (or direct) reinforcements, such as sweets or extra outings.

There is evidence that well-organised token economy systems do promote desirable behaviour, particularly in an institutional setting. However doubts have been raised regarding the long-term effectiveness of such programmes and about whether the effects are due to reinforcement or to other variables.

Behaviour therapy   Behaviour therapy is a term usually applied to techniques based on classical conditioning which deal with involuntary or reflex behaviour. It aims to remove maladaptive behaviours and substitute desirable ones. One example of such a technique is **systematic desensitisation**, which is mainly used to remove phobias. For example, a patient who had an irrational fear would first be taught to relax. Gradually the feared object would be introduced to the patient in a step-by-step process until the patient could tolerate actual contact with the object without anxiety. (See Chapter 3, Section II for an account of the way behavioural therapies are influenced by beliefs associated with environmental determinism. See also Chapter 6, Section III for a consideration of some of the ethical issues surrounding the use of behavioural therapies.)

Evaluation of the Behaviourist Approach

The behaviourist approach is a dominant influence in psychology. It represents one of the 'hardcore' approaches which has contributed a great deal to our understanding of psychological functioning and has provided a number of techniques for changing unwanted behaviour. Its use of rigorous empirical methods has enhanced the credibility of psychology as a science. (See Chapter 6, Section I for a discussion of behaviourism in relation to the scientific method.) Criticisms of the approach include the following:

1. Its mechanistic views tend to overlook the realm of consciousness and subjective experience and it does not address the possible role of biological factors in human behaviour.
2. Individuals are seen as passive beings who are at the mercy of their environments. This emphasis on **environmental determinism** leaves no room for the notion of **free will** in an individual. (See Chapter 3, Section II for a more complete discussion of the issue of free will and determinism.)
3. Its theories of classical and operant conditioning cannot account for the production of spontaneous, novel or creative behaviour.
4. Its basis in animal research has been questioned (see Chapter 6, Section II on the use of animals in psychological research).

5. Clinical psychologists who adopt behaviourally-oriented ther-apies have been criticised for treating the probable symptoms of mental disorders whilst often ignoring possible underlying causes.

Self-assessment Questions

1. What, according to the behaviourists, is the most important influence on the development of behaviour?
2. What do you understand by 'behaviour shaping through succes-sive approximations'?
3. Give an example of the use of the technique of behaviour modification.
4. Briefly explain how Skinner applied the principles of operant conditioning to programmed learning.
5. Briefly evaluate the behaviourist approach.

SECTION IV   THE COGNITIVE APPROACH

The cognitive approach contrasts sharply with that of both the psychoanalysts, with their emphasis upon the importance of the unconscious mind, and the behaviourists, who focus largely upon the links between external events and behaviours. Cognitive psychologists believe that the events occurring *within* a person must be studied if behaviour is to be fully understood. These internal events, often referred to as **mediators**, since they occur between the stimulus and the behaviour, include perception, thinking processes such as problem solving, memory and lan-guage. Unlike psychoanalysis and behaviourism, the cognitive approach does not espouse a single body of theory, and no single theorist has predominated in the way that Freud influenced psychoanalysis and Skinner behaviourism. What cognitive psycho-logists have in common is an approach which stresses the import-ance of studying the mental processes which affect our behaviour and enable us to make sense of the world around us. Thus cognitive psychologists may ask questions such as: How do we remember? Why do we forget? What strategies do we use to solve problems? What is the relationship between language and thought? How do we form concepts? There is a general belief that cognitive processes operate not randomly but in an organised and systematic way. The human mind is therefore often compared to a computer and human beings are seen as **information processors** who absorb information from the outside world, code and interpret it, store and retrieve it.

The influence of the cognitive approach can be seen also in many other areas of psychology. Thus one might talk about a cognitive approach to moral development or a cognitive theory of emotion.

Methods of Study

Clearly the processes that cognitive psychologists study are not directly observable: one cannot lift off the top of an individual's head and observe memory at work! However it is recognised that insights into mental processes may be inferred from an individual's behaviour, provided that such inferences are supported by objective, empirical data. Therefore the experimental method, with its emphasis on objectivity, control and replicability, is popularly used. Some examples of experiments which may be encountered in the area of cognitive psychology are as follows:

1. **Gregory** (1972) in his study of perceptual illusions investigated participants' perception of the Muller–Lyer figure and the Necker Cube. His findings indicated that, when the figures are removed from their flat paper background and represented as luminous figures suspended in the dark, they are perceived as three-dimensional. This finding contributed to Gregory's theory as to why people are 'taken in' by such illusions.
2. **Neisser** investigated **feature detection theory** (FDT) in his research into **pattern recognition**. FDT maintains that patterns such as letters of the alphabet are made up of a number of basic features such as vertical lines, curves and diagonal lines. For example, the letter T may be analysed as one horizontal feature and one vertical feature. Recognition of letters involves the brain in detection of these basic features.

   In a series of well-known experiments, Neisser (1964) presented participants with tasks requiring them to search through lists of letters in order to locate a pre-specified letter placed in various different positions in the lists. He found that participants located the letter A much more quickly in lists made up of rounded letters such as O, Q and G than in lists containing angular letters such as N, E and W. This confirmed the hypothesis derived from FDT that, the fewer the common features between the target and non-target letters, the more quickly the patterns are analysed by the brain.

3. **Loftus** studied some of the effects of memory on eye-witness testimony. She was testing the hypothesis that memory is reconstructive in nature; that is, our memory for events is often unreliable in that we sometimes reconstruct the past in line with what we believe *could* or *should* have happened. This process, Loftus believes, can be greatly influenced in a court setting by the kinds of questions witnesses are asked.

   In one of her experiments Loftus (1979) showed three groups of participants a film of a car accident. One group were asked to estimate the speed of the cars when they hit each other. A second group were asked an identical question but with the words 'smashed into' substituted for 'hit'. The remaining participants were used as a control group and were not asked to estimate speed. Findings showed that the 'smashed into' group estimated speed as significantly higher than that estimated by the 'hit' group.

Models in Cognitive Psychology

As already noted, one of the difficulties facing cognitive psychologists is that of attempting to study processes which are not directly observable. Hebb (1949) proposed some clear guidelines as to how this problem might be partially dealt with. He suggested that, in order to study information processing by the nervous system, it was not necessary to have a precise knowledge of the brain and its functions. Until firm physiological evidence was available one could propose hypothetical (or possible) **models** of the way some aspects of the nervous system – for example that relating to memory – might operate. A model could then be tested by experimental or other means and in the light of research findings might be adapted or replaced by a new model.

The use of models in cognitive psychology has proved a valuable and fruitful means of gaining information. There follows a brief account of some models which have been developed and tested in cognitive psychology.

The Broadbent Filter Model of Selective Attention

This model represents an attempt by Broadbent (1958) to explain how the nervous system selects some stimuli to pay attention to while ignoring others. The model, which focuses on the processing of auditory information, proposed that a filter exists, very early in processing, which is attuned to the physical features of the incoming stimuli. These are passed through for higher processing in the brain whilst other unattended information is filtered out and lost. (See Chapter 5, Section I for further explanation of this model.)

Later models of selective attention were proposed by Treisman (1964a) and Deutsch and Deutsch (1963). The latter model was revised by Norman (1976).

Atkinson–Shiffrin Two-Process Model of Memory

Atkinson and Shiffrin (1971) proposed a model which illustrates the relationship between short-term memory and long-term memory (see Figure 2.1). A central feature of this model is its emphasis on the role of **rehearsal**, which has two main functions: to maintain incoming information in STM, and to transfer information from STM to LTM. The notion of two memory processes has received much research support. However other models have also been proposed, the most significant being that of the **levels or depths of processing model** (Craik and Lockhart, 1972).

Computer Simulation of Human Thinking

With the advent of the computer, many computer programmes have been developed which have attempted to model human thinking. This approach is known as computer simulation.

Perhaps the most famous of these programmes is the **General Problem Solver**, devised by Newell, Shaw and Simon (1958) and Newell and Simon (1972). This programme attempts to simulate the strategies used in human problem solving. It proposes that much human problem solving is heuristic; that is, it is based on the

FIGURE 2.1
Atkinson-Shiffrin Model of Memory

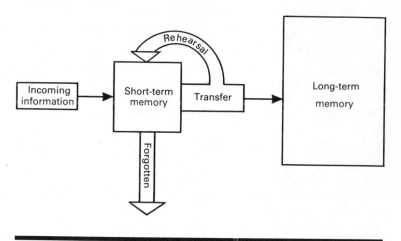

testing of intelligent 'hunches'. Newell *et al.* support this heuristic model with evidence derived from participants thinking aloud about the strategies used as they worked on problems.

As more sophisticated programmes have been devised in order to simulate human thinking a controversial debate has developed. Some critics question the whole premise of likening people to machines. Others argue that computers can do only what they are programmed to do, and that we do not yet know enough about the way the human brain works to be able to reflect its activity in computers.

Cognitive Development

A brief word should be said finally about the work of psychologists who have studied cognitive development. The most significant of these is **Jean Piaget**, who has made a monumental contribution to our understanding of the development of logic and concept attainment from childhood to maturity. **Jerome Bruner**, also, has made an outstanding contribution to an understanding of cognitive development in children. An account of these two theories and some of their practical applications can be found in Birch and Malim (1988).

Evaluation of the Cognitive Approach

The cognitive approach emphasises the importance of mediational processes, such as perception and thinking, which occur between a stimulus and a response. Research carried out by cognitive psychologists has aided our understanding of these processes. Practical insights have also been offered into such issues as how memory may be made more effective and how to improve problem-solving skills.

A problem with the cognitive approach lies in its lack of integration. Though 'cognitive theories' exist in many different areas of psychology, no single, coherent theory links these areas into an identifiable framework. For example, in addition to theories of perception, memory and thinking, we refer to cognitive theories of emotion, cognitive dissonance and social cognition, but the descriptions and terminology used tend to vary in each area. This lack of integration may exist in part because of the lack of a single important theorist, as noted earlier.

The information-processing metaphor drawn from computing and emphasising 'man as a machine' has offended some psychologists. They point out that the computer analogy fails to recognise the most fundamental differences between humans and machines: people forget, computers do not; people are emotional and irrational whilst computers are logical and unable to feel emotion.

The wide use of the experimental method in cognitive psychology has been criticised, largely because findings are said to be 'artificial' and not in keeping with behaviour and events occurring in the 'real world'. It is suggested that people's behaviour may be influenced by the setting and by characteristics associated with the experimenter. (See Chapters 4 and 6 for a more complete evaluation of the experimental method.)

Self-assessment Questions

1. Why is the cognitive approach often referred to as an 'information-processing' approach?

2. Outline some of the questions explored by cognitive psychologists about human mental activity.
3. What do you understand by the term 'model' in cognitive psychology? Give an example.
4. Consider the main strengths and limitations of the cognitive approach.

SECTION V   THE HUMANISTIC (OR PHENOMENOLOGICAL) APPROACH

For many years psychology was dominated by two great schools: the psychoanalysts with their emphasis on instinctive, irrational human beings influenced by the contents of an unconscious mind (see Section II) and the behaviourists, who viewed humans as mechanistic beings controlled by the effects of the environment (see Section III). Towards the middle of the twentieth century, a third great force appeared which offered a view of the human being as a free and generous individual with the potential for growth and fulfilment. This third force gave rise to the **humanistic** approach. Humanistic psychologists believe that psychology should be concerned with the subjective, conscious experience of the individual. They emphasise the uniqueness of human beings and their freedom to choose their own destiny. They regard the use of scientific methods as inappropriate for the study of human beings. A major aim of psychology, they believe, should be to help people maximise their potential for psychological growth.

The humanistic view is optimistic. Humans are seen as striving to achieve their potential – to achieve the maximum personal growth within individual limitations. Two leading exponents of the humanistic approach are Carl Rogers and Abraham Maslow.

Carl Rogers was a clinical psychologist and, like Freud, developed many of his views through his work with emotionally troubled people. During this work he observed that many psychological problems arise from what he called the **would/should** dilemma. This refers to the conflict between what people believe they ought to do (shoulds) and what they feel is best for them (woulds). For example, an individual may feel that he/she would like to get on with some important work at the office, but should spend more time with the family. The discomfort caused by the would/should dilemma results in anxiety.

Rogers's theory of the human personality started from the premise that people are basically good. Each individual is unique and has a basic need for **positive regard**; that is, to have respect and admiration from others. All people, Rogers believed, are born with the **actualising tendency**, a motive which drives us to grow and develop into mature and healthy human beings. Central to the theory is the concept of the self, the person's view, acquired through life experiences, of all the perceptions, values and attitudes that constitute 'I' or 'me'. This **perceived self** influences both the individual's perception of the world and of his/her own behaviour. The other aspect of self, according to Rogers's theory, is the **ideal self**, one's perception of how one should or would like to be. Thus a woman might perceive herself as successful and respected in her career but with certain shortcomings as a wife or mother (which might or might not be true). Her ideal self might demand that she be equally successful in both these spheres of her life. Good psychological health exists where the perceived self and the ideal self are relatively compatible. It is when there is a serious mismatch between the two or between the self and experiences of the real world that psychological problems arise.

Rogers developed a form of **client-centred therapy** in which the clients (not 'patients') have the power and motivation to help themselves, given the right circumstances. The facilitator (not 'therapist') attempts to create a warm, accepting atmosphere in which this can happen. Unlike the situation in other kinds of therapy, the facilitator is not an expert, authority figure and the therapy is non-directive. The aim is to help clients clarify their thoughts on problems to gain greater insight into them. This greater understanding helps the client to recognise his/her own strengths and limitations and is very often accompanied by an increase in self-esteem. Along with this, a clearer understanding of constraints which are real, as opposed to imagined or self-imposed, can eventually help the client to decide how to act. The key factor in Rogerian therapy is that the client becomes more in control of his/her fate and finds satisfactory solutions to problems. The facilitator does not offer a judgement on the appropriateness of the client's solutions,

Rogers and other humanistic psychologists often use a group

setting for therapy. Group therapy, they believe, allows individuals to express their problems openly to others and the feedback they receive also provides valuable insights about how they are perceived by others.

Abraham Maslow. Both Rogers and Maslow believed that self-awareness and the ability to come to terms with oneself are necessary ingredients for psychological well-being. Both also see human beings as striving to achieve their potential – to achieve the maximum amount of personal growth possible within their individual limitations. However, where Rogers emphasised the importance of the self-concept, Maslow was greatly concerned with the motives that drive people.

Maslow believed that there are two kinds of motivation: (a) deficiency motivation, the need to reduce physiological tensions such as hunger and thirst, which may be seen as correcting inadequacies; and (b) growth motivation, which has to do with the satisfaction of needs such as the need to be loved and esteemed; growth motives operate on the principle that, when no deficiencies remain, people have the need to develop beyond their present condition.

As Maslow studied motives in a wide variety of situations he noticed that they tended to fall into a specific pattern which could be arranged into a hierarchy (see Figure 2.2). Maslow's **Hierarchy of Needs** has become almost synonymous with his name. He believed the needs in the hierarchy to be inborn and present, at least initially, in all people. Lower needs, such as those for satisfaction of hunger and thirst, must be at least partially satisfied before needs further up the hierarchy become important. Maslow viewed the motive towards **self-actualisation** – the need to find self-fulfilment and realise one's full potential – as the pinnacle of achievement in the satisfaction of needs.

Evaluation of the Humanistic Approach

The humanistic approach has served the valuable purpose of forcing psychologists to take account of the subjective experience of the individual and the importance of self-esteem in psychological functioning. Its insistence that the scientific method as presently conceived in psychology is an unsatisfactory vehicle for studying subjective experience has encouraged psychologists to

FIGURE 2.2
A Representation of Maslow's Hierarchy of Needs (after Maslow 1959)

look for more appropriate methods. In summary, humanistic psychology represents an important counterbalance to the more deterministic approaches which have dominated psychology for most of the twentieth century.

In a practical sense, humanistic psychologists have done much to advance methods of assessing self-concept and of developing

therapeutic techniques which encourage self-respect and autonomy in individuals. The main criticisms of humanistic psychology
centre on the following:

1. That (as with psychoanalysis) its terminology is not clearly
   defined and therefore not easily testable. However Rogers
   himself has called upon psychologists to investigate some of his
   ideas. Also he and his colleagues have contributed to
   psychotherapy research by tape-recording therapy sessions and
   making them available for analysis by researchers. Some empirical studies have been carried out using the Personal Orientation Inventory (Shostrum *et al.*, 1976) which claims to be a
   measure of self-actualisation.
2. The client-centred therapy advocated by Rogers has some
   limitations. For example, it seems to be most successful with
   people who are more articulate and who are motivated to seek
   help. Clients who are withdrawn or seriously disturbed may
   need more direct help in changing their behaviour.
3. Some have criticised the values espoused by humanistic psychologists. The view has been expressed that the theories of Rogers
   and Maslow place too much emphasis on the well-being of the
   individual at the expense of concern for the welfare of others
   (Wallach and Wallach, 1983).
   (See Chapter 3, Sections II and IV for an examination of the
   humanistic position in relation to the issues of freedom v. determinism and idiographic v. nomothetic approaches. See also Chapter 6, Section I for a discussion of humanistic psychology in
   relation to the scientific method.)

Self-assessment Questions

1. Outline the most important ways in which the humanistic
   approach differs from other approaches.
2. Briefly describe the main aspects of Rogers' theory of human
   personality.
3. What is 'client-centred therapy'?
4. Give a brief account of Maslow's 'hierarchy of needs'.
5. Evaluate the humanistic approach.

WHICH APPROACH?

The details of the five approaches outlined above will become clearer as you encounter them in greater depth in your wider study of psychology. The conflict of ideas and beliefs between these different approaches may seem confusing and you would be forgiven for asking 'Which is the right approach?' However it is important to realise that no one approach contains the whole truth about psychological functioning. Each focuses on different aspects of human behaviour or experience and, as such, may be seen as complementary rather than competing. Indeed many psychologists working in practical situations feel free to select from different approaches those ideas which seem most helpful to the particular situation in which they are operating.

Psychology is a young discipline relative to other sciences. As such, it has no global **paradigm**, or single accepted theory, about the nature of human beings in the way that biology is influenced by Darwin's theory or physics by Newton. Until this is possible in psychology, the scope and variety of the many different approaches allows us to adopt different **levels of explanation** in order to explain human functioning.

Levels of Explanation

It is possible to describe and explain an aspect of human functioning in many different ways. The following example should help to illustrate this fact: the simple act of shaking hands when you meet an old friend could be described and explained from many different perspectives:

1. It could be reduced to an account of the neural and muscular activities which occur (physiological approach).
2. It might be seen as an activity which is the result of previous conditioning processes; that is, it has been associated with rewards or reinforcement and is triggered by an appropriate stimulus, in this case meeting an old friend (behaviourist approach).
3. It could be argued that thought processes are important. Your purpose in shaking hands is to demonstrate to your friend that

you remember him well and still hold him in high esteem (cognitive approach).
4. Psychodynamic explanations could be introduced. Physical contact with someone you previously found attractive may affect your emotional state (psychoanalytic approach).
5. The need for acceptance and approval by others may be seen as an important variable (humanistic approach).

Many other perspectives or levels of explanation might also be employed. For example, social and cultural factors most certainly play a part in the act of shaking hands. Whilst some psychologists concentrate their efforts on one particular approach, many others are happy to draw upon a number of different levels in their attempts to describe and explain human behaviour and experience.

Self-assessment Questions

1. What is the value of having many different approaches to the study of psychology?
2. Think of your own example which may illustrate the use of different levels of explanation.

FURTHER READING

J. Medcof and J. Roth (eds), *Approaches to Psychology* (Milton Keynes, OU Press, 1979).
H.L. Roediger, J.P. Rushton, E.D. Capaldi and S.G. Paris, *Psychology*, 2nd edn (Boston/Toronto: Little, Brown, 1987).

REDUCED TO MANAGEABLE PROPORTIONS,
HE'S MUCH EASIER TO STUDY !

Philosophical Issues in Psychology   3

At the end of this chapter you should be able to:

1. define, describe and evaluate 'reductionism';
2. define 'determinism' and 'free will';
3. make an evaluation of 'free will' and 'determinism' and explain where psychoanalysis, behaviourism and humanism stand on this issue;
4. trace the development and make some evaluation of the questions of 'nature' and 'nurture' in psychology;
5. define, describe and evaluate the terms 'idiographic' and 'nomothetic' as applied to psychological research;
6. define and explain what is meant by 'consciousness' in psychology;
7. describe ways in which psychologists have attempted to account for motivation and identify the strengths and weaknesses of these attempts; and
8. describe and evaluate ways in which psychologists have explained emotion.

INTRODUCTION

One of the reasons why modern psychology seems such a fragmented discipline is that the different approaches take up different positions on a number of key philosophical issues. This not only affects the basic view of the nature of human behaviour, but also dictates how research should be conducted and how the findings should be applied.

In this chapter four of these issues will be addressed: reductionism, determinism and free will, nature and nurture, and idiographic and nomothetic approaches. Additionally Sections V, VI and VII will discuss the issues of consciousness, motivation and emotion, which are of key importance throughout psychology.

SECTION I   REDUCTIONISM

The basic idea of reductionism is that some complex phenomena can be explained by breaking them down into separate, simpler parts. Reductionism claims that the chosen level of explanation is the only one needed to give a full account of behaviour. In psychology this has been done in four different ways.

Physiological Reductionism

Because human beings are biological organisms, physiological reductionism means that all actions, perceptions, thoughts, feelings, memories and disorders can be explained using **neurophysiological** concepts. The advantage is that all kinds of behaviour can be described in concrete and concise terms and so are susceptible to scientific methods of research. Thus it becomes possible to predict, understand and control behaviour and therefore to fulfil the aims of psychological science.

Examples of Physiological Reductionism

Recent discoveries have shown a physiological basis for some mental disorders, such as depression and schizophrenia. This has increased the hope that such disorders may be eradicated by physiological or chemical treatments.

Memory loss, pain, addiction, delinquency and even the extent of sex-stereotyped behaviour in humans (Peele, 1981) have been claimed to have physical explanations. Thus there is a kind of 'hoped for' reductionism – that physical explanations will eventually be found for all behaviour. Few psychologists would subscribe to the view that this exclusively physiological reductionist approach is desirable.

Biological Reductionism

Hebb (1974) advocated biological reductionism: human behaviour can best be understood through the study of less complex animals. Ethologists, such as Lorenz (1966), who put forward a theory of human aggression from his observations of different animal species, and sociobiologists also subscribed to this kind of reductionism. Other examples include comparative studies of animals which throw light on such diverse human behaviours as attachment, communication, territoriality, dominance, sexual behaviour, monogamy, learning and parenting.

A problem with biological reductionism is that it assumes an **evolutionary continuity** of behaviour between men and animals. Not all psychologists accept this. This is further discussed in Chapter 6, under the heading of 'animal experimentation'.

Experimental Reductionism

Experimental reductionism attempts to reduce behaviour to models showing its components and the relationships between them. For example, radical behaviourist reductionism explained all behaviour in terms of 'stimulus–response' connections.

Westland (1978) suggests that any research which looks at one aspect of behaviour rather than the whole person is reductionist. For example, measurement of personality or intelligence without reference to people's emotional or motivational states, their social or cultural background, or the test conditions, will not provide a complete explanation of behaviour.

Another example is provided by laboratory investigations into social phenomena such as conformity or obedience (see Malim and Birch, 1989, Chapter 4) which may not tell us much about the whole person's behaviour outside the experimental situation.

Experimental reductionism may make psychologists vulnerable to criticisms that all they do is pull habits out of rats, or that psychology is no more than the science of the young US white male undergraduate. Perhaps this is the price psychologists must pay for greater precision and scientific status of precisely defined terms and carefully controlled research strategies.

Machine Reductionism

Machine reductionism uses **computer simulations** to help explain such phenomena as problem solving, perception and intelligence. The computer is analogous to the brain, the programme to the workings of the mind. There have been impressive simulations created, particularly in problem solving.

Although machine reductionism can provide useful models of human cognitive functioning, there are limitations. For example, just because machines and humans produce similar outputs, this does not mean that they were arrived at in the same way.

The most difficult problem for machine reductionism is to reproduce the unique qualities which make human behaviour so unpredictable. Computer memories do not fade with time, computers do not become bored or tired, they do not think, they are not conscious and they do not exercise free will. In many ways machine analogies are probably better at telling us what humans are *not* like.

Evaluation of Reductionism

Reductionism is more compatible with the idea of psychology as a science than other, higher-level explanations. This can mean higher status and greater respectability. Scientific method seeks explanations that are as economical as possible, and reductionism contributes to this. If scientific status is desirable, then psychologists must look for the simplest level of explanation which gives a full account of human behaviour without losing vital material.

However Putnam (1973) says, 'psychology is as undetermined by biology as it is by elementary particle physics . . . people's psychology is partly a reflection of deeply entrenched societal beliefs' (p. 141). This reflects the view held by many other psychologists.

Legge (1975) explains reductionism by using the example of signing one's name. The psychological description of this would be 'He signed his name.' However the activity could be described at a lower level in terms of the muscular contractions involved. An even more specific description could be that of the brain activity which initiated the muscular contractions. An even smaller 'unit of analysis' might be that of the chemical changes involved in the brain. Legge argues that such a reductionist approach may not, by itself, be helpful or meaningful, for two reasons:

1. As the units analysed become smaller and more specific the resulting descriptions become more lengthy, complex and difficult to handle meaningfully.
2. A name may be signed with many different writing instruments and materials, from the use of chalk on a blackboard to that of a ball-point pen on a cheque. Whilst an individual's signature would retain many of its distinctive characteristics in each case, the pattern of muscle movements involved would vary and the resulting descriptions of the physiological mechanisms involved would be different.

Legge concludes that the distinguishing features of a signature arise from a pattern which is independent of the physiological mechanisms involved. Therefore a psychological account of the activity may be preferable to a longer, more complex physiological one.

Cohen (1977) says that to seek single causal explanations for human behaviour is hopeless. Behaviour is too variable and determined by too many factors. Sometimes lower-level explanations are helpful, sometimes more than one level will be necessary. Using the example of memory she says that, when people make errors of recall, it is not very helpful to explain this by saying 'they did it because they forgot'. It is more useful to talk in reductionist terms about decay of memory traces. On the subject of mental disorders, however, physiological explanations alone may be insufficient and it may be necessary to draw on social and cultural factors as well.

Peele (1981) also questions the wisdom of moving away from psychoanalytic, humanistic and non-physiological explanations towards physiological reductionism, even though it offers 'compact causal explanations' and 'holds out the promise of clear-cut remedies that would otherwise seem painfully beyond solution'. He illustrates by using examples of addiction and mental illness:

1. Addiction has been explained in physiological terms such as a genetic predisposition or lack of naturally occurring pain-relieving chemicals called 'endorphins'. In an experiment on morphine dependency in rats, Alexander *et al.* (1978) kept one group of rats in isolated and cramped conditions, and another in pleasant, roomy conditions in the company of other rats. In both groups the only liquid available for drinking was morphine solution. This continued until the rats were habituated to the morphine; then, in a series of test trials, they were given a choice between water and the original solution. Isolated rats drank significantly more morphine solution than the social rats. This demonstrated that the process of dependency is strongly influenced by social and environmental factors, not just physiological ones.

2. Another example is what is called **learned helplessness** (Seligman, 1974). It is based upon animal experiments which showed that, when rats are faced with inescapable, uncontrollable, noxious stimuli, such as electric shocks, they learn to be passive in the face of them and react by withdrawing. Similarly people who learn that they can do nothing to influence what happens to them develop helplessness and apathy and eventually become depressed. Although this can happen to both men and women, women are more at risk because of their status in society and their lack of power relative to men. Women come to depend on others for their feelings of self-worth so that they tend to blame themselves when things go wrong or when the social reinforcement they need is not forthcoming. They thus become more vulnerable to loneliness and depression.

This social psychological explanation of depression does not point to treatment by physiological means, yet drug therapy persists, as does the search for physiological explanations.

Alternatives to Reductionism

Autonomism

This is reflected in the work of Freud and of humanistic psychologists. It suggests that same-level explanations of behaviour are desirable and lower-level ones are not. Humanistic therapy, for example, focuses on experience, emotion and choice and an understanding of the world as the client sees it. Unfortunately this overlooks biological and physiological aspects of the person and so is, possibly, incomplete.

The 'Slice of Life' School

Here the idea is to study behaviour in large, complete segments to obtain as complete a picture as possible. This means a move away from experiment towards descriptive and observational methods. There is a loss of control, but a gain in realism. The problems are: what slice of life do you select? How complete can the records of behaviour be? Should you include a person's personal and cultural history? This approach is rich but very complex. It is hard to decide which of the variables observed determine behaviour and which do not.

Interactionism

This approach could incorporate biological, mechanical and social aspects of behaviour. It could include observation as well as experiment and also computer simulation. In short, all the approaches so far described would be drawn together to complement each other. There is the possibility that by this means a complete account of human behaviour could one day be produced.

In contrast with this, Rose (1976) proposes a hierarchical model of explanations of behaviour ranging from holistic assumptions of people such as sociologists to the physical explanations of physics. Psychology is placed between these extremes. Rose argues that the debate about holistic v. reductionist explanations is unimportant as each level on the hierarchy uses terminology and methods suited to itself. To use one level to help explain another is, he suggests, a fruitless exercise.

Self-assessment Questions

1. Give a general definition of the term 'reductionism'.
2. Name four kinds of reductionism and provide examples of each.
3. What objections have psychologists raised to reductionism?
4. Describe three alternatives to reductionism.

SECTION II   DETERMINISM AND FREE WILL

The determinism–free will issue is one of the oldest philosophical issues in the study of human behaviour, and one of the most pervasive. It is an importance consideration in other areas such as the mind–body issue, the nature–nurture and the idiographic–nomothetic debates, and the question of the suitability of the scientific method in psychology.

The core of the determinism–free will issue is whether human behaviour results from forces over which an individual has no control of whether it is the result of free choice. This section will examine in more detail what is meant by determinism and free will and then relate them to three major forces in psychology: psychoanalysis, behaviourism and humanistic psychology. In each case, both theoretical and practical implications will be discussed.

Determinism

This follows loosely from the work of the philosophers Locke, Berkeley and Hume, who believed that human behaviour is the result of forces over which one has no control. This applies to factors both within and outside the person.

Internal causes (**biological determinism**) include a biological need state (for example, hunger or thirst), instinctive energy or genetic endowment. Classical psychoanalysis is an example of biological determinism. External causes (**environmental determinism**) may include learning experiences or stimuli in the environment. An example might be radical behaviourism. All behaviour thus has a cause and cannot have happened any other way.

Points arising from this approach include the following:

1. The approach is compatible with scientific method, and is one of the central assumptions of this method. Determinists assume that human behaviour is orderly and obeys laws, and so is explainable and predictable. A person's current behaviour is the result of what went before and the cause of what is to come. When you know a person's history and current situation you can predict what that individual will do next.
2. If you can predict behaviour you can also control it. Knowing a person's history and current state, it is only necessary to

arrange circumstances to obtain the desired reaction. (Skinner described a Utopian society created along these lines in *Walden Two*, 1948).

3. If behaviour is determined by events outside one's control then the idea of responsibility vanishes. Neither criminal nor benevolent acts are the result of free choice, so that notions of praise and blame are worthless. To punish or reward people for certain behaviour may therefore be a pointless exercise. This has important implications for the penal system. An environmental determinist might see criminals as victims of circumstances beyond their control: it is not the criminal that needs changing but the environment. Imprisonment and various other forms of punishment might be seen to be appropriate as providing new learning experiences aimed at producing more socially desirable behaviour. If one believes in free will, punishment becomes retribution, because the criminal act is the result of free choice.

The Arguments for Determinism

1. The scientific approach is based upon determinism.
2. Science is a successful route to knowledge.
3. Therefore determinism seems to make sense – it has face validity.

Criticisms of Determinism

1. The assumption that one can ever arrive at a complete description of the current state of à person is probably not justified. To do this takes time, during which the individual has moved on.
2. It is a false assumption that accurate predictions are possible. Even physicists have to build 'uncertainty factors' into their laws. If physicists have this problem, where does that leave psychologists with their notoriously unpredictable subject matter of human behaviour? They may argue in their defence that it is not the inherent nature of the subject matter but their own lack of skill in making precise measurements which makes it difficult for them to make accurate predictions.
3. Determinism is unfalsifiable. If determinists cannot find a cause for human behaviour they assume, not that a cause does not

exist, but that they have not been able to discover one yet. For example, an advocate of free will (FW) might challenge a determinist (D) to predict what FW will do next. FW can prove D wrong by choosing not to do as D predicts. But this does not invalidate D's position because D's prediction has added another variable. FW has behaved in a different way from the way he would have done had he been ignorant of FW's prediction.

Free Will

This point of view is associated with the writings of Plato, Kant and Descartes. Descartes in particular has argued that humans are unique among living things because they have a soul. This allows them to plan and make free choices. Psychological approaches which lean most towards free will are existentialism and the more familiar branch of humanistic psychology.

Free will might logically be defined as the opposite of determinism, but this is not what psychologists mean by the term. It would mean that behaviour is uncaused, capricious and random. Experience does not support the view that behaviour is unpredictable. It is possible to discern behaviour patterns which, to some extent, do seem predictable. The position usually adopted, therefore, is not one of free will but of **soft determinism** – a term coined by William James.

Soft Determinism

This view holds that behaviour is determined by the environment, but only to a certain extent. While a person can choose between a number of courses of actions, there is only free will if there is no coercion or compulsion. Where there is consistency between a person's wishes and actions, there is an element of free will. A hard-line determinist would argue that there is no element of choice: all behaviour is caused by events outside one's personal control.

A soft determinist approach sees the problem as one of freedom v. coercion; a hard determinist approach sees the problem as one of freedom v. causation.

Summary

The free will side of the argument needs to see a person as actively responding to forces rather than being passive in the face of them. The cause of behaviour is likely to be located within the individual. Concepts such as cognition, reason and judgement would be used when a person decides how to deal with an environmental or physiological demand.

Soft determinism seems to have more face validity than either hard-line determinism or pure free will. In a society which advocates personal responsibility hard-line determinism is unacceptable and free will is difficult to define satisfactorily. If there is inconsistency between a person's desires and actions, a sense of freedom can still be achieved by changing one's desires or one's actions so that they are in line with each other.

The argument in psychology is likely to be between soft and hard determinism rather than between free will and determinism. Unless some aspects of behaviour are determined, the scientific approach cannot be justified: 'The scientist can ignore the free will/determinism question if he wishes, with the proviso that there is one extreme position – that of complete indeterminacy – which he cannot hold since it is inconsistent with his activities. No regularities, no science. The scientific view of man must therefore hold that man's behaviour is, at least to some extent, lawful and predictable' (Wertheimer, 1972, p. 31).

Free Will and Determinism in Theory and Practice

Psychoanalysis

In classical psychoanalysis the cause of behaviour is located within the individual. Behaviour is driven by powerful instinctual forces of which the individual is largely unaware. These forces are largely sexual and aggressive. The behaviour which results may be either constructive and self-preserving or destructive or even self-destructive. Behaviour originates from within, but the individual has little free choice about how to behave. Determinism holds that no behaviour is without a cause; psychoanalytic explanations therefore score highly. One of the attractions of Freudian theory is that it can deal with aspects of behaviour and experience which other approaches find it hard to explain – dreams, slips of the tongue, sense of humour and the wide appeal of great works of art are examples. Accidents also may sometimes be explained by arguing that they are unconsciously motivated. If you fall off your bicycle on your way to take your psychology exam and sprain your wrists there may be said to be an unconscious connection! Freudian theory can explain the development of personality, sex role, morality and various mental disorders. The determinist approach also has implications for psychoanalytic therapy. Every detail which the analysand is urged to divulge (thoughts, dreams, wishes: seemingly disconnected, meaningless trivial or inoffensive details) is seen as a possible window on the unconscious mind, which determines behaviour. The impression of freedom in the psychoanalytic situation is an illusion.

More recently ego psychologists, such as Karen Horney, Anna Freud and Erik Erikson, have challenged this extreme determinist view. They see the goal of analysis as 'ego strengthening'. This puts individuals more in command of their fate by making them more able to deal with the demands of reality. Horney even suggested self-analysis. (See Chapter 2, Section II for an account of the psychoanalytic approach.)

Behaviourism

Radical behaviourism is an example of environmental determinism. It is theoretically possible to predict and control behaviour by means of a full knowledge of a person's genetic limitations, past experiences and current situation. All behaviour is rational (it obeys laws) and people are therefore fundamentally alike.

Skinner (1971) rejects free will as an illusion. Only by recognising that behaviour is environmentally determined is it possible to harness the environment to create and maintain socially acceptable behaviour. In our society poorly defined, inconsistent and uncontrolled reinforcement contingencies give an illusion of freedom. We need to recognise that behaviour is already controlled; the control needs to become more systematic if Western societies are not to head for self-destruction. Freedom does not mean self-determination but freedom from aversive control. Skinner believed this can be achieved through the careful use of positive reinforcement, with minimal use of negative reinforcement and punishment.

Some critics of the behaviourist view argue that determinism and free will can be seen in the processes of learning known as classical and operant conditioning. In the former the organism is passive. The conditional stimulus produces an automatic conditional response in a machine-like manner. Clearly such behaviour is determined. In operant conditioning the organism could be seen as having free choice over which response to make. (Pavlov's dogs had no choice but to salivate to the sound of a bell but a rat in a Skinner box can choose whether or not to press a lever.) Skinner rejects this distinction, arguing that operant behaviour is determined by a history of reinforcement which affects the probability with which responses will occur. Some responses to a stimulus will have been reinforced more often than others and so are more likely to recur.

Behaviourism can also explain seemingly altruistic behaviour in animals. If conditioning determined behaviour, organisms would act only in their own interests and not be altruistic. Wertheimer (1972) gives the example of pigeons playing ping-pong. A hungry pigeon can be trained by behaviour-shaping techniques to peck a ping-pong ball off the opposite side of a miniature ping-pong table for the reinforcement of a few seconds' access to some seed. The bird, once trained, can be placed opposite an equally well-trained partner. The pigeons peck the ball to and fro until one fails to return it. Then a few seconds elapse in which the winner can feed. Then the game begins afresh. The birds become more skilled, the rallies lengthen and the opportunities for feeding diminish. At this point the birds are likely to allow the ball to fall off the table, thus allowing the other to feed. This seems to be co-operative, insightful, unselfish and therefore free behaviour. Skinner, however, argues that this is not the case. Relatively more frequent reinforcement results from allowing one's partner to win. Sharing pays better than selfishness.

Therapies influenced by the environmental determinism of radical behaviourism include:

1. Systematic desensitisation for the treatment of phobias.
2. Modification of problem behaviour in children.

3. Treatment of self-injurious behaviour through aversion therapy.
4. Development of self-care in the mentally ill by the use of token economies.
5. Cognitive behaviour therapy, such as Ellis's rational emotive therapy.

The stereotyped picture of the behaviour therapist is of one who controls a passive client, but many modern behaviour therapies encourage the active participation of the client, aiming to teach self-control and coping. One example is systematic desensitisation for phobic behaviour. Clients would develop their own hierarchy of feared situations and learn to face these with the support (not the control) of the therapist. They might also arrange their own reinforcements for positive behaviour.

Biofeedback is another example of therapy where the client is in control. A physiological measure such as pulse rate or galvanic skin response (GSR) is taken, amplified and continuously fed back to the person visually or audibly. Clients learn to control their own physiological responses. Reinforcement is the knowledge of progress made. This is useful in the treatment of headaches and nervous tension, for example.

Humanistic Psychology

This is often said to be the nearest one can get to free will in psychology. Humanistic psychologists have a problem with scientific method because it is based on the assumption of determinism and reductionism. Humanistic psychologists advocate study of the whole person and are especially critical of experimental method in psychology and of the behaviourist tradition of studying animal behaviour and then extrapolating this to humans. They view humans as unique and reject a method which removes freedom and dignity from experimental participants: if we can view animals in experiments as objects, how long will it be before we start to see humans in the same way?

Rogers's client-centred therapy reflects the view that we are in charge of our own lives and responsible for our own personal growth. Both client and facilitator are free agents. If the client chooses to allow his life to be determined by forces outside himself

he is still, paradoxically, acting freely. (See Chapter 2, Section V
for a more detailed account of the ideas of Abraham Maslow and
Carl Rogers.)

Summary

Free will and determinism are not mutually exclusive. While
humanistic psychologists lean towards free will, but still accept
that there are constraints on behaviour, determinists accept the
existence of 'uncertainty' factors. It is possible to take an entirely
environmental approach and see behaviour as externally controlled or else to argue that control comes from within the
individual, exercised by internal biological forces (hence nature–
nurture debates). If we see free will and determinism as extremes
on a continuum, then the question to be asked is not whether
behaviour is free or determined, but where on the continuum it
lies.

Self-assessment Questions

1. Distinguish between determinism, free will and soft determinism.
2. Explain where psychoanalysis, behaviourism and humanistic
   psychology stand on the determinism–free will issue and show
   how this is reflected in their therapeutic approaches.

SECTION III   THE NATURE–NURTURE DEBATE

The nature–nurture debate in psychology concerns the role of
genes and environment in determining behaviour. The nature side
of the controversy is associated with the nativists, who argue that
behaviour is (for the most part) determined by innate or inherited
factors. Environmentalists, or empiricists, are associated with the
nurture side. They would argue that behaviour is mainly determined by experience.

The empiricist position is that the baby's mind at birth is like a
blank slate (tabula rasa) on which experience will write. Behaviour
which is acquired as the baby grows is the result of experiences,
especially learning. Therefore changes in the environment pro-

duce changes in the individual. Within their physical limitations, anyone can become anything, providing the environment is right.

The nativist position is that individuals are born with an inherited 'blue-print'. Behaviours which are not already present at birth will develop as though they were on a genetic time-switch; that is, through the process of maturation. The environment has little to do with individual development and there is little anyone can do to change what nature has provided.

It follows from these two views that learned behaviours are within our control; innate ones are not, unless they are modified through genetic engineering. The question of what psychologists might be able to control and what is beyond their control occurs in many areas of research. Examples include the origin of language, personality, mental illness, aggression, gender differences and intelligence. However it is the purpose of this section to deal with the general problem of nature and nurture rather than with specific issues. The reader may be familiar with research in some of these areas and should consider its validity in the light of what is to come.

Changes in the Emphasis of the Nature–Nurture Question

The nature–nurture debate is older than psychology itself and is still as vigorous as ever. Its emphasis has altered over the years. These changes are discussed in a classic paper by Anne Anastasi (1958) and can be summarised as follows.

Which One?

At its most extreme, the nature–nurture debate asked which of the two, heredity or environment, was responsible for behaviour. Anastasi argued that to ask the question in an 'either/or' form was illogical. One could not exist without the other. Both heredity and environment are absolutely necessary for the person to exist; therefore both must exert an influence on the person.

How Much?

If it is accepted that both nature and nurture play a part in determining behaviour, how much is contributed by each? Thus the either/or question is replaced by an assumption that the two forces operate in an additive, but still separate, way: X + Y = behaviour. In Anastasi's opinion, such an attitude is as illogical as its predecessor. Even if we consider that, say, 80 per cent of intelligence is due to nature and 20 per cent to nurture, that 80 per cent still has to exert its influence in an environment and the 20 per cent can only be expressed through the organism. To ask 'How much?' is simply to ask 'Which one?' in a slightly more complicated way. It is still illogical.

In What Way?

If neither of the previous two questions is useful, the obvious answer is to consider that genetics and environment interact. The argument is as follows:

1. Genetics and environment exert an influence on each other such that X × Y = behaviour. A useful analogy is the area of a rectangle. The rectangle cannot exist unless both length and width are present, yet its area is altered by changes in either of them. Similarly behaviour is determined by both heredity and environment.
2. Different environments acting on the same genetic pattern would result in different behaviours. Similarly the same environment would produce different behaviours from individuals who were genetically different.
3. Genes never determine behaviour directly; they only do so via the environment. Likewise the environment does not directly affect behaviour but only via the genetic make-up of the individual.
4. It is thus much more logical to accept that nature and nurture interact. This raises the inevitable question, 'In what way do they interact?' How do changes in one affect the influence of the other? This is the question which now occupies psychologists.

What is Meant by Heredity and Environment?

Defining heredity and environment is not as simple as it appears. Lerner (1986) offers a solution by suggesting that we should think of environment as having different levels. (These ideas he borrowed from Riegel, 1975/6.) Anastasi elaborates her ideas further by suggesting that the influence of heredity and environment can vary from very powerful to relatively weak. The ideas of Lerner and Anastasi are summarised as follows.

Levels of the Environment (Lerner, 1986)

The inner–biological level   This refers to the environment experienced by the individual *in utero*. The influence exerted by the individual's genes can be modified by the physiological state of the mother, for example if she smokes, consumes alcohol or other drugs, has an unbalanced diet or contracts a disease, such as rubella.

The individual–psychological level   Another influence on the inborn child is the mother's psychological state. She may experience stress, which can affect the foetus differently according to when, during pregnancy, the stress is experienced.

The physical–environmental level   After birth the child may be subjected to unfavourable environmental influences, such as pollutants, additives in food, excessively noisy surroundings or overcrowding. Alternatively physical–environmental influences could be favourable.

The sociocultural–historical level   People experience unique environments which vary according to where and when they were born. The environment will be affected by the current state of scientific knowledge about what is good or bad for you. For example, educational and health care practices change with our knowledge of the effects of diet, pollution and lifestyle.

Because of socio-historical influences, cross-sectional and longitudinal investigations into heredity–environment issues are fraught with problems. Researchers are unlikely to find consistency in their results when studies are carried out on different samples, in different places and at different times.

The Continuum of Heredity (Anastasi, 1958)

If it is accepted that heredity's influence on behaviour is always indirect (via the environment), how does this influence operate? Anastasi considers that the influence of heredity operates along a 'continuum of indirectness', meaning that, at one extreme of the continuum, influences are 'least indirect' while at the other they are 'most indirect'. She gives examples of indirect influence from four points along the continuum.

Hereditary influences which resist environmental change These are at the 'least indirect' end of the continuum. However they are not entirely independent of environmental influences because heredity needs an environment in which to express itself. Down's syndrome is a good example of this level of influence. Given our current state of knowledge, it remains a problem which cannot be 'cured'. However future scientific advances in chromosome technology might enable scientists to deal with such genetic abnormalities antenatally.

Hereditary defects that can be changed by the environment These move a little further towards the 'most indirect' end of the continuum. Babies born with hereditary defects such as deafness and/or blindness fall into this category. Such defects can retard social and cognitive development considerably unless special training is given. Dramatic examples of this are provided in the stage play and film, *Children of a Lesser God*.

Inherited susceptibility It is conceivable that individuals inherit predispositions to develop certain diseases, disorders or capabilities which will only appear if the environmental conditions are favourable. Examples might be heart disease or some mental disorders, such as schizophrenia. At this point on the indirectness continuum, two people with the same genotype could be influenced quite differently by different environments.

Social influence Towards the 'most indirect' end of the continuum lie social influences on heredity. An example of this lies in social stereotypes. People may be stereotyped on the basis of inherited physical characteristic, such as hair colour, body build or sex. This could lead to certain expectations about the abilities and behaviours which go with the stereotype. For example, if someone who is genetically female encounters a stereotype which holds that females are not very academic, it is likely that she will encounter a different educational and social environment from one in which no such stereotype exists. She may even grow into the expectations which society has of her through a mechanism known as the **self-fulfilling prophecy**. In this way hereditary influences can be altered by social forces.

The Continuum of the Environment (Anastasi, 1958)

Environment also can exert different degrees of influence on behaviour (at whichever of Lerner's levels we choose). Anastasi sees environment as influential according to a continuum of breadth. This means that environmental influences, operating via the person, can have very narrow and specific effects or very broad and general effects on behaviour. Anastasi offers two types of environmental effect.

Organic effects The environment can bring about physiological (organic) changes in a person through either damage, disease or enrichment. Long-term use of alcohol, for example, can bring about a variety of physiological changes which have a very broad effect on behaviour. A disease such as polio can have very general effects. Other diseases, such as chicken pox, have relatively narrow and short-term effects. Enrichment of diet in children may have very broad effects on their intellectual functioning, though this may only affect specific aspects of intelligence test performance.

Stimulative effects Stimulative effects exert a direct influence on behaviour which, again, can be broad or narrow. Broad stimulative effects include such things as social class, through which a person may be exposed to experiences different from those in other social classes, in terms of lifestyle, expectations, opportunities and material wealth. Narrow stimulative effects involve relatively short-term experiences, such as receiving a particular type of schooling or being fostered by a particular family. (The reader might like to consider educational enrichment programmes such as 'Project Headstart' in the light of these ideas.)

The Nature–Nurture Debate in Perspective

The writings of Lerner and Anastasi cited above show just how complex the nature–nurture debate has become. To add to this complexity, Lerner points out that, potentially, there are an infinite number of different environments. In addition it is estimated that there are over 70 trillion potential genotypes (genetic types). (Even identical twins who share the same genotype have different environments from the start, since they occupy different points on the placenta.) Further to this, recent genetic research seems to suggest that genetic endowment does not place fixed limits on an individual and that even some genetic characteristics are flexible. Given that this infinite number of environments will interact with the enormous number of potential (and possibly flexible) genotypes to produce behaviour, it might be tempting to give up research into such a vast problem at this point! However it is still possible to go on to consider the second question in the nature–nurture debate: 'How do heredity and environment interact?'

How Do Heredity and Environment Interact?

In trying to answer this question, Anastasi and others have used the concept of 'norm of reaction'. Rather than seeing the genotype as a kind of blue-print for development, Anastasi prefers to think of it as something which sets upper and lower limits. There are a number of potential outcomes for individuals within the range of their genetic limitations and this is the 'norm of reaction'. Which one eventually develops will depend on the interaction of their genes with a particular environment.

A famous example provided by Hebb (1949) on intelligence illustrates the norm of reaction idea. The genetic upper and lower limit to intelligence makes up Intelligence A. Intelligence A interacts with the environment so that some or all of it is realised. This is known as Intelligence B. However the usefulness of 'norm of reaction' is limited. For example, there is no way of measuring Intelligence A or B. Intelligence tests are not the answer as they can only assess a portion of Intelligence B. (This portion is known as Intelligence C – see Figure 3.1 (Vernon, 1969).) Also they may attempt to draw on parts of intelligence A which have not yet developed. However in many aspects of behaviour, including intelligence, there is often no way of assessing what potential could be expected even when the genotype (which could be flexible) is known. It has to be accepted, therefore, that in most cases the norm of reaction, as an explanation of heredity–environment interaction, is limited.

FIGURE 3.1
The Hebb/Vernon Model of Intelligence

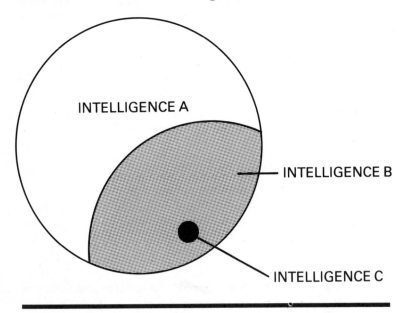

Conclusions

In conclusion a number of points may be made:

1. Given the potential variability in genotypes, coupled with the

infinite variations in environment, the inevitable conclusion is that no two individuals (even identical twins) are alike.

2. It follows from (1) that it is nonsense to look for general laws of behaviour which are couched in environmental terms (as in radical behaviourism, for example). Instead it would make more sense to look for individual laws which can explain a person's unique developmental pattern. Nativists must at least accept the influence of the 'norm of reaction' and even, perhaps, the idea of flexible genotypes.

3. An item of animal research will serve to illustrate the complexity of the current state of affairs. Various strains of pregnant mice were subjected to a variety of environmental stressors, such as swim tanks, noise and so on. Their offspring were then compared with the offspring of controls. The experiences of the mother while pregnant had different effects on the behaviour of the offspring but these effects varied according to both the genotype of the mother and that of the offspring. Here the mother's genotype interacted with her environment and that influenced the prenatal environment of the offspring, which interacted with its genotype to produce the final behaviour (De Fries, 1964).

4. If the insights from De Fries's study were thought of in human terms, individuals' behaviour is also likely to be influenced prenatally. They will also experience different social, cultural, domestic and scholastic environments. How does this affect something like educational policy? According to the norm of reaction argument, each person needs individual attention in a uniquely tailored environment. However, in practice, it is more usual to adopt the view that everyone deserves the best, no one should have more advantage than another and what is best for one is best for all. Passionate arguments develop about selection and streaming in education and about which school a child should attend. It should be borne in mind that a so-called 'better' environment is not ideal for everyone. This is, of course, just one narrow application of the nature–nurture question. The reader will doubtless think of many others.

5. Recent developments in genetics now suggest that the idea of a 'norm of reaction' must be modified and that genetic endowment is more flexible than was previously thought. Rigid upper and lower limits to development may not exist.

Self-assessment Questions

1. Identify three stages in the development of the nature–nurture debate.
2. Describe four levels at which the environment might operate to influence behaviour.
3. Describe four points on the 'continuum of heredity' and two points on the 'continuum of environment'.
4. How do environment and heredity interact?

SECTION IV   IDIOGRAPHIC AND NOMOTHETIC APPROACHES

Most major philosophical issues in psychology were around long before the subject was recognised as a separate discipline and the idiographic–nomothetic approach distinction is no exception. Those who take the idiographic approach think that it is preferable to attempt to understand human behaviour through in-depth studies of (presumably unique) *individuals* and to develop laws which apply only to one case. Those who take the nomothetic approach say it is more useful to study *groups of people* (who presumably have things in common) in order to establish laws of behaviour which are generally applicable to all. The conclusion drawn about whether psychology should be idiographic or nomothetic has important implications for its status as a science since, it has been argued, idiographic methods are characteristic of the arts, while nomothetic ones characterise the sciences.

The idiographic–nomothetic debate has its origins in nineteenth-century Germany, where it was argued that there were important subject matter differences between the social sciences and the natural sciences and that they should be studied by different methods. In the case of the social sciences the method recommended was *Verstehen* (understanding). For the natural sciences experimental, quantitative and statistical methods were more appropriate, leading to explanation, prediction and control. It was Windelband who first used the terms 'idiographic' and 'nomothetic' to describe this distinction and Allport (1962) who first applied them to psychology (although, later, he changed the terms to 'morphogenic' and 'differential', which he felt were more fitting).

Of the three major 'forces' in psychology, behaviourism leans towards the nomothetic approach while psychoanalysis and humanistic psychology (of the latter of which Allport is considered a founding father) are idiographic. (See Chapter 2 for a discussion of the psychoanalytic, behaviourist and humanistic approaches.)

Idiographic and Nomothetic Approaches in Practice

The idiographic–nomothetic distinction is most commonly encountered in the field of personality. Is it better to study an individual intensively so that by gaining a full understanding we will be able to predict that individual's behaviour at different times and in different contexts or should we try to discover general underlying traits which all people have to some extent? In the latter case, personality could then be measured on some predetermined scale and it would be possible to say what people in general would probably do at different times and in different situations. Such an approach is much more compatible with science than is an idiographic one. The idiographic approach suggests that people are unique and aims for a complete picture of an individual's personality, while the nomothetic selects certain key features of the person through measurement.

The case study is perhaps the best example of the idiographic approach. Lazarus (1971) quotes a well-known example by Allport (1965) which concerned a woman known as 'Jenny'. As case material, Allport used 301 of Jenny's letters which she had written over a period of eleven years. From these he was able to pinpoint recurring themes and construct a picture of her personality. Many other examples of the use of case studies in research can be found. Freud based his theory of personality development on several clinical cases, including that of Little Hans, through which he developed his ideas about infantile sexuality, the Oedipal conflict and castration anxiety. Outside personality theory, Piaget (1953) kept a diary on the intellectual development of his own three children. Gardner and Gardner (1969) investigated the possibility that non-humans could acquire human language by teaching sign language to a chimpanzee (Washoe). In an attempt to throw light on the development of visual perception, Gregory and Wallace (1963) studied the progress of a 52-year-old man, known as 'SB', who had regained his sight after over 50 years of blindness. All these studies, and more, have an important place in psychological literature and in many cases they have formed the basis of powerful theories.

Allport recommended other kinds of idiographic technique which were useful in personality research. One example is 'matching', in which correlations between a variety of kinds of personal expression, such as handwriting, handshake and voice are examined. Another example is that of questionnaires which are specifically designed for the individual following intensive interviews and can be used and re-used during the course of therapy as a means of monitoring progress. Semi-idiographic measures include Kelly's repertory grid technique for personality assessment and the Q-sort for measuring changes in self-concept during therapy.

Nomothetic research includes anything which involves studying groups of individuals in order to discover laws of behaviour. Radford and Kirby (1975) say these laws can be of three kinds:

1. **Classifying** people into various groups in order to predict how they might behave in certain circumstances. In clinical settings, different kinds of mental illness can be classified, which helps in predicting the chances of success of various treatments.
2. Establishing **principles** of behaviour which will apply to people in general, for example cognitive dissonance in attitude change or punishment and reinforcement in learning.
3. Establishing **dimensions** on which people can be placed and compared to one another using some kind of standardised test. Examples are the Eysenck Personality Inventory, which aims to measure two major personality dimensions (extraversion/introversion and neuroticism/stability) and the Wechsler Intelligence Scales, which measures IQ.

An example of nomothetic research quoted by Lazarus comes from Hetherington and Wray (1964) who were interested in the effect of alcohol on people's acceptance of aggression. Using questionnaires, they identified participants who were either high or low on two dimensions – aggression and social approval. Half the participants in each of these four groups were given an alcoholic drink. Participants were then exposed to aggressive cartoons and asked to rate how funny they were. One of Hetherington and Wray's main findings was that, under the conditions with no alcohol, participants who scored high on both personality measures found the aggressive cartoons much less funny than did other participants, but the introduction of alcohol to such a group resulted in an increase in their ratings of funniness. The alcohol seemed to disinhibit participants who were aggressive, yet needed social approval.

The above piece of research has all the features of a nomothetic approach. It isolated two major variables and manipulated them in carefully controlled situations to produce data which could be analysed in terms of group scores. Such findings should be generalisable to others who differ in their levels of aggressiveness and need for social approval. The research comes close to being able to predict the behaviour of individuals, but its conclusions are still in general terms; that is, in the form of statistical probabilities. The idiographic approach, on the other hand, puts individuals in classes of their own through the use of flexible, unstandardised procedures.

Advantages and Drawbacks of Idiographic and Nomothetic Procedures

Nomothetic Approach

The most obvious advantage of this approach is that it allows for the generalisation of findings from samples of participants to populations. This is because the emphasis is on precise measurement, carefully controlled investigations and replicability, and it deals with the general rather than the particular, which makes the approach more scientific.

Drawbacks relate mainly to difficulties in prediction and the loss of the 'whole person' and can be summarised as follows:

1. It is difficult accurately to predict the behaviour of individuals. Nomothetic research only leaves us with the probabilities and how useful these are depends upon one's needs. It is of little interest to the individual that there is a one in 100 chance of becoming a schizophrenic. It is more important for that person to know whether the condition will actually develop. The

health services, however, may find such data extremely useful in planning the provision of health care.

2. Nomothetic research ignores the 'whole person'. Individuality is lost the moment the person becomes a statistic in a sample. Allport points out that different people could be classified as the same personality type after scoring the same on a personality test, but they may have scored on completely different items from each other. However Radford and Kirby claim that psychological tests of personality, or general laws of behaviour, may not be precise but they are a close psychological fit and will not be too wide of the mark.

3. Psychological tests are based on concepts such as personality and intelligence, which are created by psychologists. Whether they are psychologically 'real' in the sense that measurements in inches are physically real is another matter.

Idiographic Approach

Idiographic research addresses the wholeness and uniqueness of the individual and aims to give a complete and in-depth picture. This is fine if it is these unique qualities which are important. If it is not, then shortcomings exist:

1. Findings from individuals do not usually tell us anything about others. Generalising from a sample of one is an extremely risky business. (This is one reason why replication of research findings is so important.) However case studies do have a place in scientific psychology. They are particularly useful when the study is long-term and likely to involve expensive procedures, as in the case of Washoe. Also, as Dukes (1965) pointed out, many case studies have been 'like the single pebble which starts an avalanche' in terms of advances in theory (for example, Piaget's work).

2. Idiographic studies do tend to be somewhat subjective, intuitive and impressionistic and it can be difficult to establish which variables are important and which unimportant in establishing a person's behaviour.

Idiographic and Nomothetic Approaches Working Together

Can idiographic and nomothetic approaches be seen as complementary, or is one more important than the other? A number of points may be made:

1. A truly unique person would be unrecognisable and it is clear that people do have some things in common. Allport in his later work spoke of 'traits' which people have in common and 'personal dispositions' which are peculiar to the individual. He set about the apparently contradictory task of developing a trait theory which would still take account of uniqueness. Allport has encouraged psychologists to address the task of devising new idiographic methods of research. To this extent he has been important in bringing the person back into psychology.

   In 1962, Allport and Holt entered a spirited debate on the merits of idiographic and nomothetic methods. Holt argued that the idiographic approach is not science but art. Like the arts, it attempts to create pictures of uniqueness in which understanding the individual is the key issue. The science of psychology should be nomothetic. Allport's reply is that idiographic and nomothetic approaches must work together. Neither is sufficient on its own: solely idiographic approaches give too global a picture of someone, while nomothetic ones are too general. One is needed to balance the other.

2. Falk (1956) argues that both idiographic and nomothetic approaches are part and parcel of the scientific method. If the aims of science are to describe, understand, predict and control, then idiographic methods apply best to the first two and nomothetic approaches to the latter two. Idiographic approaches are helpful in new areas of research where new variables are being discovered and nomothetic ones are to be preferred when more precise definitions of them are required.

3. Eysenck (1966) suggested the idiographic–nomothetic problems could be solved by a compromise. He warned of the importance of not neglecting the role of subject variables in research. He suggested that, at the very least, experiments should have 27 types of participant, who between them would cover all possible combinations of the following: high, medium and low intelligence; high, medium and low extraversion; and high, medium and low neuroticism. Analysis of the resulting data could then take into account individual differences between participants. It should be noted that, while Allport would probably welcome the spirit of Eysenck's views, he is

critical of the idea of using a limited number of predetermined psychological dimensions which might have little relevance to the individual.

4. As the nomothetic approach has been so powerful in psychology in recent decades, it is understandable, as Pervin (1984) says, that 'there is an effort to bring the person back into personality research without, however, relinquishing the goal of systematic, general principles of psychological functioning' (p. 268). As Lamiell (1981) puts it, there is an interest in **idiothetics** – an approach which attempts to capture the best of both worlds. This is a philosophy which will eventually affect many areas of psychology, not just the field of personality theory from which it has sprung.

Self-assessment Questions

1. Distinguish between the terms 'idiographic' and 'nomothetic', giving examples of illustrative research.
2. Describe the strengths and weaknesses of nomothetic and idiographic approaches to psychology.

SECTION V   CONSCIOUSNESS

In 1890, William James wrote, 'The explanation of consciousness is the ultimate question for psychology.' His words remain true to this day and psychologists are still perplexed by a number of related questions. What is consciousness? Where is it to be found? What are its functions? Do animals have consciousness and, if so, is it like a human's? How does consciousness develop – is it present prenatally or does it appear some time after birth? Can humans create machines without consciousness? Do we have an unconscious mind? Is consciousness just one thing or several? What happens to it when we die?

No other experience is so obvious to oneself as one's own consciousness and yet it is impossible to prove the existence of consciousness in others. It is not publicly observable and therefore not scientifically testable. We can convince ourselves of our own consciousness through introspection, but we can only infer its existence in others since they can only be observed from the outside. However consciousness is not entirely alone in this way. Many cognitive functions such as memory, attention and perception are inferred from observing people's behaviour. In fact psychologists are inclined to ignore the difficult question of what consciousness is, preferring to get on with the business of studying it in its various forms. Thus the area of consciousness research covers such diverse topics as waking and sleeping, dreaming, arousal, attention, subliminal perception, biofeedback, electrical stimulation of the brain (ESB), split brain research and altered states of consciousness (ASCs) such as meditation, hypnotic states, hallucinations and drug-induced states.

Consciousness and Psychology

In recent times, consciousness has waxed and waned in popularity amongst psychologists. For the very first experimental psychologists, the structuralists, conscious experience was the very stuff of psychology. Freud happily acknowledged different levels of consciousness when he spoke of the conscious, pre-conscious and unconscious minds. Radical behaviourists rejected consciousness as unsuitable for psychological study, preferring to relegate it to a 'black box'. Cognitive and physiological psychologists made it their business to study the contents of this 'black box', while humanists adopted the study of ASCs as a rich source of information about human experience.

What is Consciousness?

A term most often used as synonymous with consciousness is 'awareness'. Some psychologists have tackled the problem of defining consciousness by trying to describe it. Others have attempted to study the nature of consciousness either by offering descriptions or by using specific methods.

Descriptions

James (1890) spoke of the 'stream of consciousness' – a kind of internal monologue which is always present. We are aware of external events through the combined information from all our senses, yet we can switch and channel attention to heighten awareness of certain aspects of the external environment. James also suggested that we have 'co-consciousness', or a number of distinct selves which are normally unaware of each other. These may manifest themselves in dreams or under hypnosis.

Methods

Early psychologists, such as Wundt, developed the technique known as introspection, in which participants were trained to describe their own mental images, sensations and feelings. Freud investigated the unconscious mind through free association and analysis of dreams. More recently a variety of methods have appeared. Some of these are described below.

EEG Electroencephalographic (EEG) recordings enable us to identify types of alertness, relaxation states and four stages of sleep. With each of these comes decreasing responsivity to external stimuli. EEG measures are taken by placing electrodes at various positions on the scalp to pick up different kinds of electrical activity.

Electrical stimulation of the brain (ESB) It has long been known that messages are transmitted around the brain and nervous system by electrochemical means. In the 1950s, it was found that it was possible to stimulate parts of the brain into action through the direct application of tiny electrical currents via microelectrodes. In this way some thought they had discovered centres for primitive emotions and drives such as pleasure, pain and hunger. Penfield (1975) went on to suggest that consciousness resided in the thalamic nuclei of the higher brain stem, since removal of the cortex does not mean loss of consciousness while removal of the higher brain stem does.

While knowledge in this area is still rudimentary, it is nevertheless possible to imagine a situation in which people's behaviour, and levels of consciousness, could be controlled robot-fashion through remote stimulation of the brain. If this were possible the case for consciousness being physiological in origin would be strengthened.

Split brain studies Generally speaking, each hemisphere of the brain is responsible for functions on the opposite side of the body to itself and some functions, such as language, seem to be located more in one hemisphere than the other. In spite of this, we do not experience two separate consciousnesses but a single unified one. It is likely that this is because the two halves of the brain are linked by a band of nerve fibres known as the corpus callosum. During the 1960s, Philip Vogel cut the fibres of the corpus callosum in epileptics and succeeded in reducing both the severity and frequency of epileptic seizures. Later research into the side-effects of the treatment revealed that patients appeared to have two different kinds of consciousness, each unaware of the other. However what this reveals about consciousness in people without such brain damage is limited. Consciousness could be located virtually anywhere in the brain and may involve other parts of the nervous system too. It could be the result of a complex network of interactions involving the normal brain and the body as well. On the other hand, it might not be physiologically based at all.

Altered states of consciousness (ASCs)   Humanistic psychologists assert that, in order to understand people, it is essential to study the content of conscious experience. Discovering new ways of making sense of the world and a deeper personal understanding can enable people to achieve their potential and, ultimately, to 'self-actualise'.

The term 'ASC' is meant to apply to any state of awareness which differs from that normally experienced. In most cultures, ASCs are encouraged and, sometimes, prized and various 'informal' ways of inducing them have been developed. In Western culture the most usual techniques involve alcohol, caffeine, tobacco, music or changes in surroundings, although ASCs can also be experienced during illness. Other cultures may be more inclined to use meditation, chanting or potions. Experimentally the following have been studied.

- *Drugs*. Masters and Houston (1966) interviewed users of mind-changing drugs such as LSD. Ethical considerations aside, such drugs have also been administered experimentally to volunteers so that their effect can be studied under carefully controlled conditions. In some cases the researchers claimed that the drug-induced state was a 'transforming experience' which resulted in changes beneficial to the person.

- *Sensory flooding and sensory deprivation.* Masters and Houston devised a technique of bombarding (flooding) a person with visual and auditory stimuli in order to alter their level of awareness. Lilly (1977) subjected himself to an extreme form of sensory deprivation by immersing himself, naked but for a respiratory mask, in a tank of water kept at a constant 93°F. He reported experiencing many different levels of consciousness. Lilly claimed that this immersion experience deepened his personal awareness and was 'a fertile source of new ideas'.

- *Meditation.* Transcendental meditation involves the use of a special 'sound' known as a mantra. Other techniques involve focusing all one's attention on a task. Practised meditators claim that the process helps them to become calmer and more aware, yet with renewed energy. Such subjective feelings are, however, hard to evaluate, so research into meditation has tended to concentrate on physiological effects, such as brain activity and other bodily functions. Brain waves associated with relaxation (alpha rhythms) do indeed increase during meditation. Heart and respiratory rates decrease and there is a general decrease in arousal in the sympathetic nervous system, which is the division most active when under stress. However some researchers maintain that similar beneficial effects could be achieved through altered lifestyle or diet.

- *Hypnosis.* The hypnotic state occupies an uncertain position between sleep and wakefulness. Under hypnosis, participants can be induced to behave in bizarre ways, but they appear to be totally unconcerned about this. That hypnosis really is an altered state of consciousness is very difficult to demonstrate, but it has been suggested that it may involve a split of consciousness into several levels of awareness, one, or a number, of which the hypnotist can tap into. Researchers into hypnotic anaesthesia have succeeded in splitting consciousness into two levels – one which experiences pain and the other which does not. However, like other ASCs, hypnosis is still only measurable by physiological means which may only give us a partial picture of what is involved.

What are the Functions of Consciousness?

It has been suggested that consciousness has the following two functions.

Choice of Action

Where a number of actions are possible, different ones can be compared and evaluated mentally without the risk or time which trying each one out would entail. This can happen consciously, though much decision making seems to occur at an unconscious level, for example where reflex actions are involved, as in driving. On the other hand, behaviour sometimes seems to cause consciousness; for example, people encouraged to smile more often rate themselves as happier than do people who are encouraged to frown.

The Monitoring and Modification of Behaviour

Consciousness could function to monitor external events and continuing behaviour and to change the latter if the strategy originally chosen did not seem to be working out. Thus behaviour can become flexible and quickly adaptable to different situations. This monitoring function could also have survival value, since it would mean that awareness could be shifted if one's well-being were under threat, for example if, while studying, you were to smell burning.

Conclusion

It should now be apparent that the nature of consciousness is still not well understood, in spite of the fact that there is good physiological and behavioural evidence to bear out the existence of different levels of awareness. There is also a wealth of descriptive material on what it is like to experience different levels of consciousness. We also know that behaviour can occur without consciousness; therefore there may be an evolutionary aspect to it whereby the more advanced a species the more awareness and levels of awareness it has.

Because of the personal nature of consciousness, it is said not to be accessible to scientific study, but it is important to remember that many such 'unobservables' are already tolerated in psychological research and theory. This is particularly true in cognitive psychology where much 'mental activity' is explained through the use of experimental evidence and models (see Chapter 2, Section IV).

There is no reason to suppose that consciousness could not, eventually, be explained in the same way and it could therefore be scientifically studied to the same extent as other mental phenomena. As with them, the focus is shifting away from the idea that consciousness is a 'thing', to be located and described, to the idea that it is a product of the dynamic interaction between the individual and the external world.

Self-assessment Questions

1. How have psychologists attempted to define and study consciousness?
2. What are the functions of consciousness?

SECTION VI   MOTIVATION

Motivation theorists attempt to explain two things: why people behave and why their behaviour takes one form rather than another. This section attempts to describe and evaluate the approaches psychologists have taken to this issue.

The Psychoanalytic Approach

Freud's view of motivation was mainly that unconscious and instinctive forces drive behaviour. (See Chapter 2, Section II.) Instinctive energies – sexual and aggressive impulses particularly – build up over time, causing unpleasant tension unless a means can be found to release them. This can happen in one of a number of ways:

1. through steady and controlled expression of the energy;
2. through defences if direct expression is thwarted; or
3. through a sudden explosion of repressed energy.

Behaviour is mostly, though not entirely, to do with tension reduction.* Other influences on behaviour include the need to deal with guilt and the immediate demands of the environment, and a person's own developmental history – especially psychosexual experiences in childhood.

Thus behaviour is psychically but multiply determined, and all behaviour can be explained in some way. It is never irrational or haphazard.

Evaluation of the Psychoanalytic Approach to Motivation

Advantages

1. The most remarkable thing about Freud's view of motivation is its scope. No other theory comes close to explaining so many different kinds of behaviour, including dreams, vocational choices, neuroses, fantasies and selectivity in perception and forgetting.
2. Like humanistic psychology, Freud's approach is holistic and can account for individual differences in behaviour. People behave differently because they differ in the strength of their instinctive drives and vary in their psychosexual histories, their defences and their ways of interacting with the environment. Psychoanalysis, like humanistic psychology, can provide insight into the individual case and this provides an avenue for treating people with psychological problems.

Disadvantages

1. Freud's emphasis on the unconscious as the major determinant of behaviour leaves little room for free will or individual choice of action.
2. The approach is somewhat negative, emphasising the role of conflict with unconscious forces to the extent that life is seen as a constant battle, rather than as a striving force for positive growth.
3. The emphasis on biological forces leaves little room for the influence of learning on behaviour and thus promises little in the way of life being a constructive experience in which it is

possible to undo early damage in any other way than through psychoanalysis.

4. Researchers have found it difficult to derive testable hypotheses from the theory which can be satisfactorily supported or rejected. The problem is mainly one of being able to find suitable operational definitions of the concepts concerned. Experimentation, however, is only one way of validating a theory, though it is the most favoured one. It is possibly not appropriate to attempt to validate this theory by using the scientific approach.

Homeostatic Drive Theory and Drive Reduction

In conjunction with **homeostasis**, 'drive' can explain human behaviour as primarily being driven by the need to meet physiological needs. Homeostasis is the process by which an organism maintains its physical state within certain optimal limits. Much of this maintenance is self-regulating. Body temperature, blood sugar and body fluids are mostly regulated automatically, but there are times when the body needs resources from outside to maintain the balance. The organism is then driven to behave in such a way that homeostasis will be restored – finding food or drink, cooling down or warming up.

A region of the brain known as the **hypothalamus** plays an important part in detecting tissue needs in respect of hunger and thirst. The motivation to sleep is less easily explained. Its survival function is less clear, though it has been suggested that it is necessary for the body to perform recuperative functions. It is even less easy to find a physiological basis for motivation for human sexual behaviour. While lower animals' sexual behaviour is closely regulated by hormones, in more advanced animals external stimuli play a greater part.

The behaviourist Clark Hull developed the idea of homeostatic drives into an extremely influential theory of learning which can explain why animals behave and how habits form. Many of his ideas were expressed in algebraic form – equations which could be used to predict the promptness, vigour and persistence with which an animal would pursue a course of action.

Hull's explanation of motivation combines the concepts of drive and habit. According to Hull, all drives stem from physiological needs, for example for food, water, correct temperature, rest, activity, the need to eliminate waste products and to avoid tissue damage. The organism will respond in ways which reduce these drives. The reduction of drives is reinforcing, so the behaviour associated with reinforcement is more likely to be repeated in the future – it becomes a habit. Drive reduction is a primary reinforcer and objects and events associated with it are secondary reinforcers. In this way specific needs may be learned. For example, if a certain food becomes associated with hunger reduction, next time we are hungry we are more likely to reach for it than for an unfamiliar food. A habit has formed and different habits can have different strengths.

Hull thought that drives and habits could be multiplied to give an indication of how likely an organism would be to respond: tendency to respond = habit × drive. If either habit or drive are zero, no behaviour will occur. For example, a rat will not press a lever for food if it has not acquired the habit to do so or if there is no hunger drive, but if both habit and drive have some value (strength), we can predict the likelihood of the lever-pressing response.

For Hull, then, drive is the motivating force, but how it is expressed in behavioural terms depends on a complicated interplay of different habit strengths in different stimulus situations. Later Hull added incentive to the equation, making predictions about behaviour even more sophisticated.

Evaluation of Homeostatic Drive Theory

Advantages

1. An important contribution made by Hull was the provision of precise mathematical statements about behaviour which were reasonably easy to test.
2. Although many of Hull's original ideas have now been refuted, he did much to encourage research into motivation and to improve our understanding of it. Hundreds of studies of learning were inspired by him and features of his original ideas still remain in current theories.
3. Like others, Hull drew attention to the power of the environment to influence responses but, unlike them, he attempted to

define its influence in precise terms which left little room for ambiguity.

Disadvantages

1. Homeostatic drive theory is reductionist and so is unpalatable to some critics. It is too mechanistic to explain some aspects of human behaviour. Much of Hull's research was on laboratory rats, but he still thought he could explain unique human behaviours such as moral, cultural and religious actions in drive-reduction terms. This does not seem tenable to many psychologists.
2. More specifically Hull's contention that animals will only learn if drive reduction is involved was called into question by the research of Olds and Milner. They showed that a rat with an electrode implanted in the pleasure centre of its brain will continuously press a bar for stimulation of this centre via the electrode. It will do this more frequently than it will press a bar for food when hungry, or water when thirsty. It will even prefer this self-stimulation to access to a sexually receptive female. Furthermore the rat's capacity for pleasure seems insatiable, therefore no need and no drive reduction is involved.
3. Hull would argue that attachment of the young to a parent occurs because the parent is a secondary reinforcer – that is, associated with the provision of food, water and so on – and the young animal learns to stay close to its parent because of this. Attachment theories argue that this parent–infant behaviour is innate, rather than learned, and that a social bond develops soon after birth and is a two-way process between offspring and parent.
4. Humanistic psychologists, such as Maslow, disagree with the emphasis on biological needs. Humans have, they argue, a unique set of self-actualisation needs which cannot be understood from animal research. Humans have non-homeostatic needs which cannot be explained in drive-reduction terms.
5. Hull's view leaves little room for individual differences, preferring to see all humans as governed by the same laws.
6. Drives do not go on increasing with the length of deprivation. While a hungry rat will search urgently for the food at the usual feeding time, if it fails to find it, its search will become less

vigorous. Clearly factors other than its internal state are important in determining motivation.

Arousal Theory

Dissatisfaction with drive theories has led psychologists to develop another approach to motivation, based on the idea that, rather than seeking a state of non-arousal, humans are motivated to achieve an optimal level of excitation, or a set point, which can vary from time to time depending on their biological condition. Some of the processes for achieving this set point are inhibitory and some are excitatory. They work together to achieve the correct level and there are set points for both physiological and psychological needs.

The optimal level also varies from person to person, which explains why people differ in their tendency to search out stimulation, novelty and complexity.

Evaluation of Arousal Theory

Advantage

Drive reduction theory has difficulty in explaining why people feel bored. Homeostasis is equivalent to a state of non-arousal which could be said to be the same as boredom. So why do people find boredom unpleasant? Arousal theory suggests that the optimum level of stimulation varies from time to time. Monotonous, repetitive inputs cause us to 'switch off'. Overstimulation can have the same effect. People need a certain amount of stability (homeostasis) as well as a certain amount of variability. The set point lies somewhere in between homeostasis and overstimulation, so that people sometimes seek out new experiences and on other occasions withdraw from them. Thus arousal theory can explain why humans are active, curious and seek sensations. Drive reduction cannot do this.

Disadvantage

Arousal theory still draws heavily on the idea that motivation can be reduced to physiological processes. This is a view not shared by all psychologists, as we shall see in the next section.

The Humanistic Approach to Motivation

Deficiency motivation arises from basic needs like hunger and thirst and some psychological needs such as the need for security. These needs create tension which must be reduced.

In addition there is a will towards personal growth, brought about by satisfying what are called 'meta-needs'. Such growth is not essential for survival and will only take place in the right conditions. Meta-needs include cognitive needs, aesthetic needs and the need to self-actualise. It was suggested that these needs were hierarchical, the needs at the bottom of the hierarchy being the most pressing and needing to be satisfied before those at the top (see Figure 2.2).

After basic needs, lower on the hierarchy, have been met it is possible to move up to the meta-needs. Maslow found that only about 1 per cent of healthy people achieve the top level of the hierarchy. He named Eleanor Roosevelt, Beethoven and Abraham Lincoln as self-actualised people.

Rogers's ideas about motivation arose through his 'client-centred therapy' (see Chapter 2, Section V). We all have an 'actualising tendency' which can help us to become a 'fully functioning person'. The task of therapy is to help the client towards self-growth and this is based on the belief that humans have a need to be 'one's own organism' and to achieve 'positive self-regard'. The client and the therapist, whom Rogers preferred to call a 'facilitator', enter into a partnership. The goal is greater personal insight. For Rogers the major motivational force is this actualising tendency.

Evaluation of the Humanistic Approach

Advantages

Between them Maslow and Rogers made an enormous contribution in the field of human motivation:

1. In contrast to the psychoanalytic and instinctual approaches there is less emphasis upon 'lower' motivations such as hunger,

thirst, aggression and sex. Human motivation is seen as vastly more complex. Self-fulfilment and self-enhancement are achieved in different ways by different people, and with different degrees of success.

2. In contrast with models which stress tension reduction, tension may be created as one strives for new experiences.

3. There is emphasis on the importance of the social environment (that is, relationships with other people) as a help or a hindrance to the satisfaction of needs. The humanistic approach has an interactionist flavour in which both the individual and the environment matter.

4. Motivation is seen as having both a short-term and a long-term effect on behaviour. We are not only motivated to satisfy immediate needs, but are also motivated to look at the long-term goal of self-actualisation and full functioning.

Disadvantages

1. Criticisms centre upon the vagueness of the humanistic approach and its lack of scientific status. The theory is based upon imprecise and vague constructs which are difficult to put to the test. It is hard to evaluate the applications which have sprung from them. However Rogers made great efforts to show how client-centred therapy might be evaluated and Maslow's hierarchy has been applied successfully in the field of management.

2. There is criticism that the wholeness approach is at the expense of the scientific aims of the control and prediction of behaviour, which can only be achieved with a more reductionist approach. However this holistic approach is also a strength. Maslow is one of the few theorists to draw together physiological, psychological and social needs into one theory of motivation. Criticisms of lack of scientific rigour are not particularly damaging to humanistic psychologists. This is the very view they are seeking to combat.

Cognitive Motives

Some motives do not seem to be based upon physiological needs but appear simply to be part of being alive. These **cognitive**

motives include curiosity and the need for achievement. Behaviour is explained as being the result of someone's thought processes or interpretation of the information around them.

Curiosity

Curiosity is unusual in the field of motivation in that it seems to have no goal other than the actions which make it up and is an arousal-provoking rather than an arousal-reducing set of behaviours. Both animals and humans show a tendency to explore and manipulate objects and situations as if to see what will happen. Berlyne (1960) conducted experiments with undergraduate college students and concluded that novelty, complexity, intensity and change were most likely to arouse curious behaviour, so that we have an urge to explore aspects of the environment which have these characteristics. Berlyne also feels that these principles can be related to the acquisition of knowledge.

It is possible that curiosity has a survival value. An animal which has familiarised itself with its environment through exploration may be better able than an unprepared one to respond effectively to problems of escaping from danger, finding food or meeting other members of its species with whom to mate.

Achievement Motivation

McClelland *et al.* (1953) referred to our need to attain success or some standard of excellence as **need for achievement** (nAch). Atkinson (1964) developed this idea by adding a related motive, **fear of failure**. Achievement motivation is thus the result of the interplay of these two forces. Much research ensued as the ways of measuring nAch and fear of failure were developed. Atkinson's research, for example, suggested that people who have higher nAch than fear of failure choose tasks of intermediate difficulty; those with higher fear of failure than nAch choose tasks either of high or low difficulty. Another line of research suggests that the lower achievements of women are not due to lower nAch or innate differences in ability but to cultural pressures. Better understanding of the cognitive processes behind the decisions of women to behave in one way or another might help the cause of equal opportunities.

Evaluation of the Cognitive Approach

1. This approach offers an explanation of motives, not easily achieved in physiological terms, but which is such an enduring feature of humans' (and some animals') behaviour that it cannot be ignored. The acceptance of the possibility that we do some things simply for the sake of it rather than for any 'pay-off' is more compatible with the view that humans are active selectors and interpreters of information rather than passive puppet-like responders to external or internal pushes.
2. The cognitive approach also allows for individual differences in the way in which individuals respond to the same situation. They select and interpret information in their own unique way. For example, two students of A level Psychology of equal ability may each need to achieve a Grade B result; the one is bored by the subject and finds it a struggle; the other is fascinated by it and thoroughly enjoys it. While the need and the drive are the same, the interpretation of the situation is different, leading to different feelings about and approaches to the subject. Other explanations do not go as far as cognitive ones to explain these differences.

Conclusion

None of the approaches to motivation described above offers a complete explanation of why people behave. However each has something of worth to offer. Theories differ mainly in the emphasis they put on the forces which underlie behaviour; that is, whether we are internally or externally 'pushed', whether motivation is in response to innate or learned forces, whether it is conscious or unconscious, mechanistic or cognitive. In fact the field of motivation is a reflection of the state of present-day psychology. If theorists agreed on why people behave, they would be able to define psychology itself.

Self-assessment Questions

1. What is motivation and why is it important that psychologists explain it?
2. Outline the different explanations of motivation offered by psychologists.

3. What are the strengths and weaknesses of psychological explanations of motivation?

SECTION VII   EMOTION

William James, in 1884, posed the question, 'What is emotion?' Over a century later there is no coherent answer. However there are several lines of theorising which can help us understand the various components of emotional experience. Many writers compare motivation and emotion, as different kinds of basic feeling which help direct behaviour towards goals. Atkinson *et al.* (1985) suggest that, while motives are internally caused, emotion is usually a response to an external stimulus. Emotions invariably activate the autonomic nervous system; motives may not. There are also differences in the subjective experience of feeling, emotion or motivation which lead them to be treated as separate, though related, phenomena.

It is generally agreed that emotions involve five components:

1. Physical changes – especially arousal or depression of the autonomic nervous system.
2. Subjective experience – feeling or 'affect' varying in intensity and in pleasantness/unpleasantness.
3. Cognitive aspects – awareness and appraisal of the situation as positive or negative.
4. Emotionally expressive behaviours – postural and/or facial changes.
5. Behavioural consequences – a response to the source of the emotion.

Different approaches have emphasised one or a combination of the above components. None has integrated them all.

Biological Aspects of Emotion

We have all been aware of physiological changes when experiencing emotion. These changes are brought about by the autonomic nervous system (ANS) which is not under our voluntary control.

Its two divisions, the sympathetic and parasympathetic, normally operate in a complementary fashion to control bodily functions of which we are generally unaware, such as respiration, heart rate and digestion. In times of stress the sympathetic division rouses us to action, increasing the rate of respiration, dilating the blood vessels, increasing the blood pressure, redirecting blood from the digestive processes to the muscles and ensuring that the blood clots more easily. These reactions prepare us for 'fight or flight' and are often accompanied by feelings of 'butterflies in the stomach'. The parasympathetic division of the ANS depresses these bodily functions so that the body returns to normal. Emotions such as fear or anger seem to arouse the sympathetic system; in sadness and grief the parasympathetic division predominates.

Theories of Emotion

James–Lange Theory (1885)

James (1884) and Lange (1885, translated 1967) proposed that bodily changes were foremost in emotional experience: we perceive a threat; the nervous system, muscles and glands react immediately. It is only after this that we perceive ourselves as being afraid, angry and so on (see Figure 3.2).

FIGURE 3.2
James–Lange Theory of Emotion

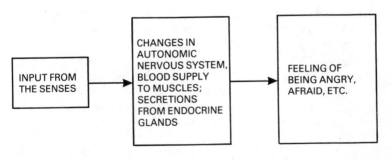

Evaluation of the James–Lange theory of emotion   Cannon (1927) and Bard (1934) criticised James–Lange on three grounds:

1. The James–Lange theory assumes that feelings of emotion are dependent upon sympathetic activity, but those with spinal injury or disease still experience emotions though they do not receive full feedback about bodily changes.
2. Sympathetic changes are relatively slow to occur, while emotional experience is not. Emotional experience therefore seems to come before bodily changes.
3. The same physiological changes can occur in different emotional states.

Cannon–Bard Theory of Emotion

The Cannon–Bard Theory of Emotion states that both the hypothalamus and the thalamus are involved in emotion. The hypothalamus controls the bodily responses; the thalamus is responsible for experience and the two systems operate independently (see Figure 3.3).

This approach has suffered from weaknesses similar to those of the James–Lange theory. Damage to the thalamus or hypothalamus does not appear to leave a person unable to behave emotionally or feel emotion.

Ekman *et al.* (1983) have been able to provide evidence that emotions can be distinguished at a physiological level. Ekman coached participants to produce facial expressions for particular emotions and to hold them for ten seconds while he measured various autonomic changes, such as heart rate and skin temperature. He found that heart rate was faster for negative emotions, such as fear, anger and sadness, and slower for happiness, surprise and disgust. Some emotions, then, do seem to be distinguishable at a physiological level. This does not mean that all emotions are distinguishable in this way. While this may weaken Cannon's third criticism of James–Lange, it does not negate it, and in any case the other two still hold.

Cognitive Labelling Theory

Schachter and Singer (1962) set out to investigate the influence of

FIGURE 3.3
Cannon–Bard Theory of Emotion

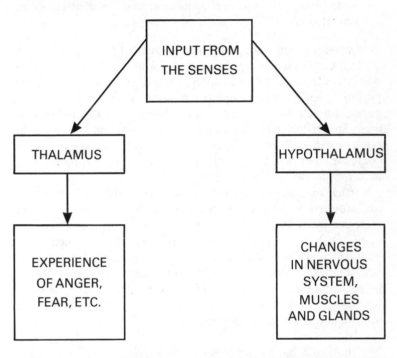

cognitive factors in emotional experience because they saw that emotion involved more than physiological changes. They told all the participants that they would be receiving an injection of 'suproxin' which would improve their performance on tests of visual perception. In reality they were divided randomly into four groups:

- 'Adrenalin informed' participants were correctly informed of the effects of the adrenalin injection, so that they were prepared for the usual symptoms of sympathetic arousal.
- 'Adrenalin misinformed' participants were told to expect slight numbness and itchiness.

- 'Adrenalin uninformed' participants were told that there would be no side-effects.
- 'Control' participants were given an injection of a placebo (an inert saline solution) and again told that there would be no side-effects.

Half of each group were told to wait patiently for a period of time, while the other half were shown into a waiting room where there was a confederate of the experimenters. Half experienced this person as behaving in a euphoric manner, making missiles out of paper and generally being frivolous. The other half witnessed an angry stooge who complained about the experiment and about the questionnaire which both he and the real participant had to complete. The stooge eventually crumpled up the questionnaire and stormed out of the room.

Participants were assessed by observers and by self-report. Misinformed and uninformed groups were more likely to take their cue from their surroundings, so that the degree of anger or euphoria they reported was higher than for the informed group who had a ready explanation for their physiological experience. Schachter and Singer concluded that emotional experience is partly determined by physiological changes, but the process of labelling and appraising one's experience using other available information is at least as important.

Criticisms of Schachter and Singer's Research

Criticisms include the following:

1. Artificiality: it certainly was not a natural situation and adrenalin is not the only physiological factor involved.
2. Pulse rate alone was used as a measure of physiological arousal. There should perhaps have been a combination of psychological and physiological measures.
3. The methods used to compile indices of anger or euphoria are also open to question (an observer's rating of the degree to which participants joined in with the stooge's antics, together with self-report.)
4. Anger and euphoria are not really comparable emotions. They differ in duration and in the amount of activity involved.
5. There have been few satisfactory replications of the experiment.

6. Perhaps most importantly, the experimenters did not succeed in manipulating physiological arousal and cognitive arousal independently. Any injection is going to be accompanied by some emotional response. In addition the results of an injection of adrenalin would not have been neutral affectively, particularly for the group which had been misinformed as to the likely results.

Attribution Theory

Schachter and Singer's work has led to suggestions that we can exercise greater control over our emotions than was hitherto thought to be the case. Attribution theorists see this control as depending upon our attribution of cause to physiological experiences. Valins (1966) suggested that awareness of physiological arousal lends us to search for the cause of that arousal. He invited male college students to look at a series of slides of semi-nude women. They were given false feedback as to their autonomic responses. Pre-recorded sounds were described for half the group as their own pulse, and for the other half as extraneous sounds. For half the participants of each group the rate of sounds increased while half the slides were presented; for the other half it decreased. Then the students were asked to rate the attractiveness of the women they saw. Those participants who had been told that they were hearing their own pulse sounds rated as more attractive the slides of those women which had been accompanied by increased rate of sounds. This did not happen for the other group, who had been told that the sounds were extraneous noise. This **Valins effect**, as it has become known, indicates that the causes which we attribute to events have much to do with our reactions to them.

There are still some aspects of emotion which other theories find it hard to explain. Attribution theory cannot explain why some of our emotions seem to be beyond our control – or why some people deliberately seek out emotionally arousing situations.

Opponent Process Theory

Opponent Process Theory (Solomon and Corbit, 1974) helps to explain both of these phenomena. The central idea is that of homeostasis – explained in the previous section on motivation in relation to physiological balance. Homeostasis is also said to operate at a psychological level. An experience of a strong emotion such as fear is always followed by an opposing emotion (relief); at first this is weak, but as exposure to the situation is repeated it strengthens. At the same time the dominant emotion weakens until it is overtaken by the opposing one. Solomon and Corbit illustrate this with the example of sky-diving. The first dominant emotion is fear, and the opposing emotion of relief is relatively weak. With successive jumps the fear emotion weakens and the relief grows stronger until it overtakes fear altogether. In the end people indulge in risky activities not because they are hooked on the fear but because they enjoy the high of the relief that follows it.

Solomon and Corbit extend this theory to explain drug addiction and tolerance. Initial contact with the drug produces a rush of pleasure and euphoria, followed by an opposing state of withdrawal and craving. With repeated doses the craving overtakes the ever-weakening feeling of euphoria. So the addict takes greater and greater doses to avoid the lows. The addiction is therefore a matter of avoiding the lows rather than achieving highs.

Positive Emotions

In *The Psychology of Happiness* (1987) Michael Argyle describes how physiological, psychological and environmental factors can combine to give positive emotional experiences. On the physiological level he says that the key to experiencing positive emotions lies in the stimulation of pleasure centres in the brain (discovered by Olds and Milner, 1954). In humans pleasant sensations of taste, sexual arousal, relaxation, enjoyment and laughter can all be evoked by stimulation of different parts of the brain (Rolls, 1979). In addition the neurotransmitters, dopamine and noradrenaline (which can be released by amphetamines) and the endorphins have all been implicated in sensations of pleasure. Endorphins are sometimes called nature's painkillers since they are released more when we are under stress, for example in combat or in competitive sport. Finally facial expression seems to play its part. Ekman (1985) showed how adopting a particular facial expression can help to induce an emotion or even modify its intensity. For example, if we force a smile we may feel happier and if we keep a 'stiff upper lip' we may feel less pain.

Experience of pleasant physiological sensations can be modified on a psychological level. Our emotional reactions to the same event can change according to our expectations and what we are accustomed to. For example, a pleasant event can be an anti-climax if our expectations were unrealistically heightened and constant exposure to a pleasant event can dilute its impact. Attribution of cause of emotional arousal plays its part here, too, as it does with negative emotions (Valins, 1966).

On an environmental level Argyle lists events which are associated with positive emotions. These include social events, work and leisure, music, weather and nature. The moods of other people can also be influential (as shown in Schachter and Singer's study). Positive emotions, like negative emotions, have multiple causes and a better understanding of them can be of great practical value. When people are in a good mood they are more likely to think positively and creatively, feel satisfied with life, help other people and like them more. Understanding how these qualities can be induced and enhanced could provide an effective treatment for certain kinds of depression. Argyle quotes research to show the relatively short-lived effect on mood of reciting positive statements, receiving praise, watching funny films, listening to cheerful music, recalling pleasant events, 'finding' something such as money or succeeding at a task. He suggests that systematic and regular use of such techniques might have more lasting effects on mood. An individual could be helped to draw up a personal programme of mood-enhancing events and activities and then be encouraged to engage in them more often. Therapeutic techniques can also be used to help depressed people to look at things more positively, improve their self-image, set themselves realistic goals and give up false beliefs which lead to unhappiness. They may also need to improve their social skills so that interactions with others are more rewarding. Thus the problem is treated on behavioural and cognitive levels so that recourse to drugs may not be necessary. This is only possible because of a better understanding of the mechanisms of emotion.

Conclusion: What is the Purpose of Emotions?

As so often in psychology we have arrived at a point where there are many explanations, but none complete. Each approach has something to offer. There remains the question of the purpose of emotions. It seems that they can be both a hindrance and a help to behaviour. A certain amount of arousal serves to improve performance, too much can be counter-productive (as stated in the Yerkes-Dodson law in 1908). Emotions also serve to organise and direct behaviour so that we are able to choose from a number of alternatives. Both motivation and emotion help us to stay alive but this does not mean that we are machines. The cognitive part of the process helps us to optimise survival, developing learning strategies to help us to cope with emotion-arousing stimuli in an ever-changing world. Learning self-control can be adaptive. Other questions which remain to be answered include why humans seem to have richer lives than animals, and why it is that there are individual and even cultural differences in emotionality. Can emotionality be bred into humans in the same way that it is possible to breed highly-strung animals? Individuals also seem to differ in their ability to 'read' emotions in others and this has led to the question of whether it is possible to train people in sensitivity. Finally one of the major obstacles to producing computer simulations of human behaviour has been our inability to programme machines with emotions. Is it emotion which gives humans their unique qualities?

Self-assessment Questions

1. What are the five components of an emotion?
2. What physiological changes accompany emotion?
3. Outline and evaluate the James–Lange, Cannon–Bard, Cognitive Labelling, Attribution and Opponent Process approaches to emotion.
4. Describe some of the recent research into positive emotions.
5. What is the purpose of emotions?

FURTHER READING

M. Argyle, *The Psychology of Happiness* (London: Methuen, 1987).

E.R. Valentine, *Conceptual Issues in Psychology* (London: George Allen & Unwin, 1982).

M. Wertheimer, *Fundamental Issues in Psychology* (New York: Holt, Rinehart & Winston, 1972).

I STILL FEEL WE HAVEN'T QUITE CRACKED THE PARTICIPANT OBSERVATION ANGLE.

Research Methods 4

At the end of this chapter you should be able to:

1. identify the methods used in psychological research, including experiment, observation, case study, survey, psychometric studies and the use of correlational techniques;
2. evaluate each method; and
3. describe examples of each of the above methods.

SECTION I   EXPERIMENTATION

The use of the term 'experiment' implies that the researcher is deliberately isolating and changing one factor known as the **independent variable (IV)**, in order to be able to measure or observe the effect of that change on another factor, the **dependent variable (DV)**, without the interfering influence of other **extraneous variables**. It is, of course, possible to alter the independent variable in more than one way, and to make more than one measurement of the dependent variable. An example will make this clearer.

Suppose that a researcher was interested in the problem of whether background music affects students' learning. It would be necessary first to make careful definitions of what was meant by background music (the IV) – it might be 'pop', classical, or even jazz music – and then to define equally precisely what was meant by learning (the DV) – for instance, it might be the recall of key facts from what has been studied.

Extraneous variables needing to be controlled might include:

- the effect of wearing headphones;
- how used the participants are to listening to music;
- the physical conditions – what kind of seating, lighting and so on;
- age;
- sex; and
- academic ability.

There can be different kinds of experiment, conducted in different settings: **laboratory experiments**, **field experiments** or **natural experiments**. An example of each is given below.

Laboratory Experiment

A laboratory experiment is conducted in a well-controlled environment. To take an illustration from the field of ethology, Eckhard Hess (1958) conducted a study of imprinting in ducklings. The ducklings were hatched in an incubator in a laboratory where the first moving thing the newly hatched ducklings saw was a plastic model Mallard duck on a revolving turntable. The ducklings became imprinted on the model and followed it on its circular travels. By this method Hess was able to identify critical periods after hatching when exposure to the model was most likely to result in imprinting. It was possible to control accurately the time when the ducklings were exposed to their 'mother' and to observe the onset of imprinting. The independent variable in this case was the time after hatching when the duckling was first exposed to the model, and the dependent variable was the extent to which the ducklings imprinted upon their 'mother'.

Field Experiment

This is an experiment carried out, not in a laboratory, but in the field; that is, the real world. An example comes from research into animal behaviour carried out by Tinbergen and Perdeck (1950). Herring gulls nest on the ground on cliffs or other territory near the sea. Parent birds forage for food at sea or in local scrap-heaps. When they return to their nest territory, they land and stand near their chick, pointing their beaks to the ground. The chick then pecks the parent's beak; the parent is stimulated to regurgitate food, allowing the chick to feed. It was comparatively easy for Tinbergen and his colleague to get near the chick and investigate what kind of stimulus – short of the natural one – produced the begging response in the chicks. A number of stimuli were tried: three-dimensional mock-ups of a herring gull's head, cardboard cut-outs and even a thin red rod. It appeared that what mattered was not how closely the 'artificial' stimulus approximated to the real one but a particular characteristic, in this case the red spot on the beak. Anything with red on it turned out to be an effective stimulus. In this experiment, the IV was the **stimulus** presented to the chick; the DV was the pecking **response**. Essentially, in a field experiment, the environment is a natural one – here the gull chicks were in their own nests.

Natural Experiment

In a natural experiment the setting is a natural one for the participants, and the changes in the independent variable occur naturally rather than being deliberately set up by the experimenter. It comes very close to not being an experiment at all in that the experimenter does not manipulate the IV but takes account, in the design of the study, of variations which occur naturally.

Suppose that researchers were interested in whether women tended to be more conformist than men. They might set up a hypothesis that women drivers are more likely to comply with traffic signals than men. They would observe the behaviour of both men and women at a particular crossing and count the number of each who crossed when the lights showed amber. This is a natural situation, uninfluenced by the researchers. The IV is the gender of the drivers, the DV the conformity or non-conformity of the drivers to traffic signals. The researchers do not manipulate the IV, but take account in the design of their study of the naturally occurring changes in the IV – gender of the drivers.

Strengths and Weaknesses of Experimentation

Strengths

1. *Control, cause and effect.* It is possible to achieve a very considerable degree of control by isolating one or more of the

variables to be studied and then manipulating their values in order to measure or observe the effect this has upon another variable. The experimenter aims to eliminate all extraneous variables. This will never be totally possible and the degree of control obtained will to some extent vary with the circumstances and setting of the experiment. Clearly the degree of control possible in a 'field' experiment such as Tinbergen's, mentioned above, will be less than that possible in a laboratory situation such as that of Hess. The systematic manipulation of one variable (IV) in order to observe the result of that manipulation on another (DV) makes it possible to establish a link between a **cause and effect**. Human behaviour is complex and any effect is likely to have several possible causes, but the close control of variables in an experiment makes it more likely that a link will be found.

2. *Objectivity*. Closely allied to control is the concept of objectivity. As Popper (1972) has said, it is unrealistic to expect any observation to be totally objective, that is to say free from the influences of the experimenter's values, interests, expectations and prejudices. Nevertheless objectivity is one of the aims of scientific study and is more nearly achievable with experimentation than with other methods.

3. *Replicability*. Because of the setting, particularly of a laboratory experiment, and the way in which an experimenter is able to describe in detail what has been done, it is usually easier to replicate (repeat) an experiment than other methods of study. Replication is important in that, where a study is repeated and the same results are obtained, there is greater confidence in the validity of the theory being tested.

Weaknesses

1. *Dehumanisation*. It has been claimed that the experimental method depersonalises and dehumanises the subject; even the use of the word 'subject' in place of 'person' is indicative of the attitude the experimenter tends to take. Heather (1976) claims that this gives a mechanistic view of man: 'He is regarded as something passive and inert, propelled into action only by the use of some force, either external or internal upon him ...

Human beings continue to be regarded by psychologists as some kind of helpless clockwork puppet jerked into life only when something happens to it.' The use of the term 'participant' is now preferred. In addition the controlled and contrived situation of the laboratory experiment is divorced from 'real life'. The impression that this is how people really behave is false and misleading. Other types of experimental design, however, can go some way towards modifying this. No one could claim that the herring gull chicks in Tinbergen's 'field' experiment are divorced from 'real life'.

2. *Distortion of behaviour.* In a laboratory experiment, too, there is real fear that placing participants in a controlled and contrived situation distorts their behaviour, so that conclusions drawn from such studies may be misleading. For instance, what person in real life would ever be asked to look at a series of lines drawn on a card, compare them with a 'test' line and say which was most nearly the same length? This was what Asch (1952) asked participants to do in his classic experiment on conformity!

3. *The participant's perception.* It is not only the contrived situation, but also the way in which the experiment and the part the participants are asked to play in it are perceived which alter their behaviour. In Chapter 6 of this book the way in which participants weigh up the experimental situation is described in some detail. **Demand characteristics** (Orne, 1962) may be exhibited, alerting the participants to the hypothesis being tested and causing them to change their behaviour in some way. A **single blind** technique may help to overcome the effects of the participants' expectations. This entails not revealing the true purpose of the research to participants until after the data have been collected.

4. *Experimenter's expectations.* The experimenter's expectations about the outcome of the experiment may also have a distorting effect on it. Rosenthal (1966) conducted an experiment which illustrates this. Student experimenters were asked to observe rats running through mazes and report what they found. One group was given to understand that their rats were a very bright strain; the others that their rats were dull. The rats were in fact no different from each other. The results showed that the

'bright' rats had performed far better than the 'dull' ones.

Good results obtained at the beginning of a study may also set up expectations in the experimenter which are then transmitted to the participants. But this is not peculiar to the experimental method.

The interpretation a researcher puts upon the data obtained may also be a cause of bias. It will tend to be that interpretation which will back up the theory being tested. Where data are not wholly objective this is even more likely to occur. Psychoanalytic data, collected during therapy, or phenomenological observations involving a less structured introspective technique, are subject to this problem.

A **double blind** technique may be used to control effects due to experimenters' expectations. Both the persons administering the tests and the participants are unaware of the real aims of the experiment and are only carrying out the instructions of an experimenter. An illustration will help to explain this.

In an attempt to test the effectiveness of ECT (electro-convulsive therapy) in treating depression, simulated ECT was used. Procedures were undertaken exactly as in a genuine treatment, except that no current was actually passed through the brain. Doctors administering the trial were unaware which patients had genuine and which simulated ECT. Patients too were only informed after the event. Morris and Beck (1974) reported 146 such double blind studies of ECT and other anti-depressant drug treatments involving the use of placebos – inert substances used instead of drugs. In no case was the placebo reported as being more effective than the treatment.

5. *Sampling bias.* If an experiment is one from which generalisations will be made to a wider group then the sample that is used needs to be typical of the group from which it is drawn. In many cases experimenters use students as participants because they are an easily available pool of bright, young adults who often receive a payment for their help, which further encourages them to volunteer. Volunteers have been shown by Ora (1965) to be insecure, dependent upon others, easily influenced, aggressive, neurotic and introverted. This might be acceptable if the experimenter's intention is to generalise the results to a population of volunteers, but they could not be applied to a

population of people who do not share these characteristics.
6. *Statistical inference.* Psychologists sometimes find difficulty in obtaining samples large enough for them to have full confidence in their results. They therefore use esimates of statistical probability with smaller samples. There is nothing wrong in doing this, providing that they and those who read their work are aware of the implications. It is usual to employ a criterion of 5 per cent significance; that is to say, the likelihood of the results being obtained by chance alone is equal to or less than five in 100, so that there can be reasonable confidence in the conclusion. However there is always a 5 per cent probability that the results are due to chance and there is no real effect there at all. Psychologists recognise this limitation and this is one reason why they must replicate research.

Self-assessment Questions

1. Define briefly the following terms: independent variable, dependent variable, extraneous variable.
2. List the strengths of experimental method. Write a brief comment on each.
3. List three weaknesses of experimental method.

SECTION II OBSERVATIONAL AND SURVEY METHODS

Where it is thought undesirable or impractical to intervene in an experimental way to manipulate the independent variable there is the alternative of observation.

Observation also provides first-stage data by which hypotheses may be developed which may then be tested by means of experimentation. It is clearly the case that some control is sacrificed and it is not possible to infer cause, as may be done in an experimental design, but ethical or practical considerations may make the more closely controlled method of experimentation impossible. It might not be considered desirable on ethical grounds, for instance, to interfere with the regime a mother adopts with her baby. Similarly, it might not prove practicable to conduct an experiment to examine the effect of teacher attitudes on pupil progress. It would be better to study differences in attitudes between teachers and the behaviour of pupils in their charge as they occur naturally rather than attempting to manipulate them.

Controlled Observation

Direct observation may be carried out in a laboratory in carefully controlled conditions, where it has many of the advantages, as well as some of the disadvantages, of experimentation. The main difference is that with observation there is no manipulation of the variables. The researcher simply observes and measures what is there in the situation. Here are two examples of this kind of research:

1. Research has been carried out into circadian rhythms, which are daily cycles of changes occurring naturally in the human body. There are changes in the temperature of the body, blood pressure and urine volume, and liver, kidney and endocrine gland activity which relate to a daily cycle. This activity was often found to be three to five times higher during the day than during the night (Luce, 1971). None of these patterns of activity were manipulated in these studies but, by closely observing them in a large number of individuals, researchers made general conclusions.
2. In sleep laboratories participants are allowed to sleep naturally but with electrodes attached to points on their scalps to measure the electrical activity in the brain by means of an electroencephalogram (Hartmann, 1973). The conditions are very carefully controlled.

Naturalistic Observation

Another alternative is not to bring participants into a controlled environment at all but to study them in their own natural surroundings. This overcomes some of the distortions of laboratory work, but there is loss of control, which may or may not be serious. Kathy Sylva and her colleagues used **naturalistic observation** in their study of children's play, carried out in playgroups in Oxfordshire. It was no less scientific than an experimental design might have been. Decisions had to be taken as to what categories of behaviour to observe, at what time intervals the observations were to take place, what the important features of the natural setting were and how to minimise the effects of the children's awareness of being observed (Sylva *et al.*, 1980).

Another example is the following study by Mary Ainsworth and Sylvia Bell. The experimenters were interested in examining the relationship between the responses a mother gives to her baby when it cries and changes in the pattern of crying on the part of the babies. They observed 26 babies in their own homes – a natural environment – for four-hour periods at intervals during their first year. The independent variables were the promptness with which the mother responded to the baby's crying and the type of response – picking up or cuddling. The dependent variable was the amount of crying. During the first three months of life it was found that the babies were more likely to cry when they were alone, and least likely to cry when the mother was near or actually holding the child (Ainsworth and Bell, 1969).

Participant Observation

A variant on the above is participant observation, where the researcher actually becomes part of the group which is being observed. David Hargreaves, in a study of social relationships in a secondary school, became a member of the staff for a period of a year (Hargreaves, 1967) and was able to observe the attitudes and behaviour of boys and staff in the school. Another example was that of Whyte (1955) who became a member of an Italian gang in Boston. He took part in all the activities of the gang, including the gambling and the shady political deals.

Strengths and Weaknesses of Observation

Strengths

1. Many, though, not all, observational studies are carried out in the field, where there is less chance of the kind of dehumanisation and distortion described by Heather. Careful design of observational studies can minimise participants' awareness of being observed.

2. Studies of this kind are likely to be more holistic and less reductionist than is often the case with experimental studies. Most of the studies described above deal with the total situation in which the participants find themselves and their total behaviour rather than with small elements in isolation.
3. Observations can provide hypotheses for more searching examination and so help in the first stage of the scientific process of gathering knowledge (see Chapter 6, Section I).

Weaknesses

1. *Distortion*. Some of the criticisms mentioned above in relation to experimentation also apply here. Where the study is laboratory-based the environment is an unnatural one and Heather's view that humans are being treated mechanistically still holds. There is also a fair chance that the behaviour observed will be distorted by the laboratory setting. Masters and Johnson (1966) set up a laboratory to study human sexual behaviour by means of controlled observation. It would have been hard to show that the sexual behaviour of the participants was unaffected by their being in a laboratory situation observed by research workers.
2. *Expectancy*. Strictures relating to **expectancy effects** will also sometimes apply here too, as will 'demand characteristics' so long as participants are aware of being studied.
3. *Sampling bias*. Sampling becomes even more important in observation than in experimentation and bias is still a possibility. Great care has to be taken to ensure that, as far as possible, the samples studied are typical of the population to which it is intended to generalise the study.
4. *Causality*. It is harder to imply cause in observational studies. Hargreaves (1967) observed that boys in the lower streams of the school he studied had poorer attitudes towards school, worse behaviour and lower attainment than in the higher streams. However it would be hard to attribute this to streaming rather than to socioeconomic conditions, intelligence or to a number of other possible causes.
5. *Observer bias*. Observer bias is also a problem, especially where the observations have not been carefully structured. The flexibility that results from a less structured design can also lead

to subjectivity in what is observed. Where structuring has been more carefully done, the structure itself is the result of decisions taken by the researcher which are probably not going to be 'value-free'. The Polish anthropologist Malinowski illustrates some of the pitfalls. While claiming to be a participant observer among the Trobriand islanders, he still lived in a separate hut, and his attitude was that of a superior towards inferiors so that his **participant observation** was not really participant. He also started from a Freudian position, examining the extent to which the Trobriand islanders exhibited such features of Freudian belief as the Oedipal conflict. Because he was looking for particular behaviour there was a greater chance that he would find it. Whyte also had difficulty in maintaining his dispassionate and neutral attitude towards members of the Italian gang of which he had become a part.

Survey Method

Another alternative is to use a **survey**. The researcher will normally assemble a large number of questions which are then posed to a representative sample of the relevant population. The questionnaire can either be highly structured, with fixed, alternative responses which can then be collated and analysed, or more open-ended, with the respondents able to express themselves in their own words.

An example of a survey is Rutter's *Fifteen Thousand Hours* (Rutter *et al.*, 1979). This was a survey conducted in 12 secondary schools in the Inner London Education Area within a radius of six miles. The aim was to examine how schools differed. The outcomes examined were academic attainment, attendance and delinquency. Survey methods were combined with structured interviews – which might be regarded as oral surveys – and some observation of events in classrooms. Variables which were considered as explanatory included the status and sex composition of the pupils, size and space, age of buildings and number of sites, staffing, class size and school organisation. While this was clearly a well conducted piece of research it depended upon value judgements made by the researchers as to what were likely to be the important variables.

Strengths and Weaknesses of Survey Method

Strengths

1. Surveys allow researchers to cover a great deal of ground and obtain responses from a large sample comparatively easily. Rutter's study, mentioned above, covered twelve schools in Inner London. He was able to make some examination of a large number of factors. In terms of outcomes, too, the scope was wide. He obtained data on attendance, pupil behaviour and academic results.
2. Surveys, like observations, may suggest further areas of research for more detailed study by other methods.

Weaknesses

1. *Data analysis*. There is real danger in surveys that decisions about what to look at will be influenced by considerations of ease of analysis.
2. *Memory problems*. Another problem is that of memory. Surveys frequently involve questioning people about their past behaviour or practices. It is very difficult for the respondents to be accurate and truthful.
3. *Distortions of the truth*. Much of the data in surveys is obtained by questioning the target group of people, either by using written questionnaires or through interviews. There is always the possibility, however carefully interviews and questionnaires are designed, that respondents will not answer truthfully. This may be because they wish to appear in the best light, or it may be because they are not interested enough to think carefully about their answers.

   The interviewer may also influence responses by non-verbal cues, tone of voice and so on. Several interviewers may be used, each of whom may cause different biases.
4. *Design*. Whether the method is open-ended or highly structured, there can be difficulties. In the case of the highly structured questionnaire, the structure will probably reflect the preconceptions of the compiler, and may force respondents to answer in a way which does not entirely accord with their views. A more open-ended survey, on the other hand, may lead to

much more subjectivity when it comes to its interpretation. Of course surveys deal with people's verbal responses to questions posed verbally, as well as with behaviour. There is no way you can be certain that what people say they do accords with what they actually do.

Self-assessment Questions

1. What are the main differences between experiment and observation in psychology?
2. List the strengths and weaknesses of observational methods. Comment briefly on each.
3. Describe what is meant by 'survey'. Show how the design and structure of a survey may bias the results.

SECTION III CASE STUDY METHOD

All the above methods have been what is described as **nomothetic**. That is to say, they depend upon scientific observation of a number of participants and, after analysis, arriving at principles of behaviour which apply to all of them. The distinction between nomothetic and **idiographic** approaches has been discussed in Chapter 3.

Case study is essentially **idiographic** in that it makes a detailed study of single individuals or instances of something, for example, a family. Allport (1961) has stressed that the purpose of psychology is to study individuals rather than groups and it is the uniqueness of individuals which case study seeks to observe. Furthermore many of the methods described above rest on **quantitative analysis**; that is to say, characteristics of individuals are measured and then statistically analysed. In some cases, only a few characteristics will be measured.

Case study, on the other hand, is based upon **qualitative** rather than quantitative analysis; that is, upon verbal descriptions of participants rather than upon numerical analysis. That is not to say that numerical measurement of characteristics is excluded, but the main data collected consist of description rather than measurement.

Examples of Case Study Method

Freud

Probably the best known exponent of the case study method was Freud. The method employed by him and by the psychoanalytic movement was the compilation of detailed case histories of patients treated, and it is out of these case histories that his theories of the nature of personality came.

The case of Little Hans illustrates this. Hans was the son of a friend of Freud, a doctor interested in Freud's pioneering work. Hans developed a phobia of horses, especially of being bitten by them, which made life rather difficult in an age when the streets were filled with them. Freud's interpretation was that, in Hans's unconscious mind, he harboured incestuous desires for his mother but was afraid that his father might discover this and castrate him as punishment. On a conscious level, Hans experienced his anxiety in the form of a fear of horses, which symbolised his father, and of biting, which symbolised castration. The explanation was backed up by detailed evidence. For instance, Hans particularly feared white horses, wearing blinkers and with black around the mouth. Hans had once said, 'Daddy, you're lovely, you're so white'. Hans's father had a black moustache, sometimes wore spectacles, and had often played horses with his son, with the father always as the horse and Hans as the rider. All these 'data' were carefully collected and used as evidence to support both the explanation for the phobia and also, more generally, the thesis that boys in the so-called phallic stage tended to suffer from what was termed an Oedipal conflict, after the figure in Greek mythology who unwittingly married his mother after killing his father.

Piaget

In his earlier work Piaget's theories were based upon detailed case studies of children, and he made very careful observations of their behaviour at every stage of their development.

Gregory and Wallace (1963)

In another example of case study Gregory describes a man (SB) who was born blind but who regained his sight as an adult. He describes in detail the effects of his new visual ability on cross-modal perception. In this case, SB's perception of objects had been oriented towards touch and he had some difficulty in reorienting it towards vision. Gregory describes in some detail the emotional problems that the change brought with it. When SB was blind he was happy to cross the street on his own but, after the operation, when he could see, he was so frightened of the traffic that he would no longer cross by himself. He was never able to use his ability to its fullest extent and died some three years later of depression.

Strengths and Weaknesses of Case Study

Strengths

1. Because case studies allow more detailed study of many facets of an individual case, rather than isolating a few measurable characteristics, there is a greater chance of gaining insights into the nature of behaviour which might be missed with other methods. For instance, in Gregory's study, the psychologically disturbing effect of a sudden reorientation of perception became a central feature of the study.
2. Because it is based upon description and qualitative data, rather than measurement and quantitative data, case study is not so likely as other methods to ignore those facets of behaviour which are not easily measured.

Weaknesses

1. *Generalisation*. Because case studies relate to single instances, it is not possible to generalise to other people. The results of a study are only valid when applied to that case. It is very tempting to use case studies as generalisable to similar cases, but this can only be done with the greatest caution.
2. *Subjectivity*. Case studies are subjective. They are based upon qualitative rather than quantitative analysis, as we have seen. Researchers alone decide how they are to interpret what they observe, what they include in their descriptions and what they leave out. It is, therefore, very easy to select only those observations which support the theory which is put forward. In

psychoanalysis, for instance, Freud was the sole analyst, observer and interpreter of what he observed in his patients. It is at least open to question whether this is scientific and objective observation. Popper (1972) sets as criteria for scientific study that it should be relatively **objective**, **generalisable**, **accessible** and **refutable**. It is not easy to say that data obtained through case study methods fulfil these criteria. On the other hand, there are many people who maintain that, because psychology deals with unique individuals, it should not have to meet scientific criteria.

Self-assessment Questions

1. What is the distinction between quantitative and qualitative data?
2. Describe the case study method and provide an example.
3. List one strength and one weakness of case study.

SECTION IV   CORRELATION

At this point it is useful to discuss the technique of **correlation**. While it is not a method of study in the same way that experimentation is, it is a statistical technique, widely used to assess the degree to which two things are related to each other. For instance, are people who are musical also likely to be good at maths? Are those who are intelligent also creative? While experimentation allows the differences between sets of data to be studied, correlation indicates the degree of any relationship which may exist between them.

In practice, correlation operates like this: suppose a researcher wants to find out whether there is a relationship between people's heights and their weights; that is, does an increase in height tend to accompany an increase in weight? First, measurements of height and weight would need to be collected from each member of a sample of people. Correlational analysis would then be applied to these data pairs to discover what kind of relationship, if any, existed between height and weight; that is to say, the degree to which they vary together.

Ways of Expressing Correlation

This relationship may be expressed by means of a **scattergram**. This is a type of graph on which pairs of measurements – in the above case heights and weights – are plotted. The pattern which results indicates the relationship between the measurements. Below are examples of scattergrams showing different types of relationship. In addition, a **correlation coefficient** may be worked out which expresses the relationships in figures. The maximum value of a correlation coefficient is 1, the minimum 0 and it may be either positive or negative. Here are some examples:

1. A perfect positive relationship (correlation coefficient + 1.0). In this case there is an exact match between the two sets of measurements. For example, the number of gallons of petrol you put into your car will exactly match the number of £ it costs: the more gallons, the more £, the fewer gallons, the less £.

   The scattergram looks like this:

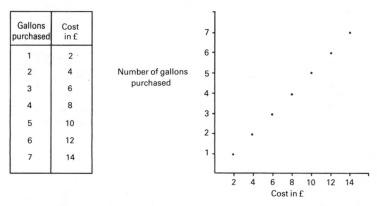

Gallons purchased	Cost in £
1	2
2	4
3	6
4	8
5	10
6	12
7	14

2. A perfect negative relationship (correlation coefficient − 1.0). Here the match is between low scores in one set of measures and high scores in the other. For example, if you were to measure the number of miles travelled and the amount of petrol left in the car at different points on a journey there would be a perfect negative correlation. The greater the number of miles you have travelled, the less petrol will be left.

The scattergram looks like this:

Miles Travelled	gallons left
20	5
40	4
60	3
80	2
100	1
120	0

Number of miles travelled

Number of gallons left

3. No relationship (zero correlation). There may be no relationship at all between the two sets of measurements. An example might be hat size and IQ. In this case, the scattergram might look like this:

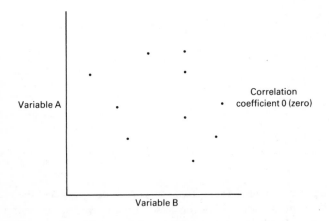

Variable A

Correlation coefficient 0 (zero)

Variable B

4. Imperfect relationships. In psychological research correlations are rarely perfect. Imperfect positive or negative correlations are expressed by decimal fractions, as in the scattergrams below:

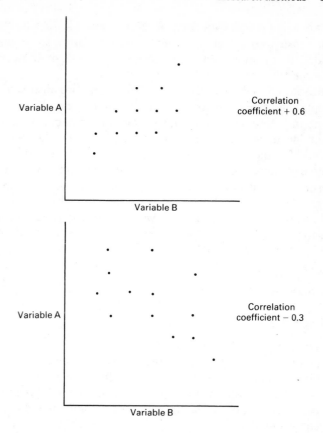

An example of an imperfect positive correlation might be the number of hours spent studying and exam grade. An imperfect negative correlation might exist between numbers of hours spent in the pub and end-of-term grade.

Correlational Studies in Psychological Research

We now consider two examples of psychological studies which have used correlation. Hill, Rubin and Peplau (1976) wished to find out the extent to which people were attracted to people like themselves. Measures of age, educational attainment, attractiveness and attitudes were taken on 200 couples, going out together, but not yet committed to each other. Correlations were carried out between the couples on each of these measures. Results showed that those who stayed together to become engaged or married tended to be more alike on these measures than those whose relationships broke up within the next year.

Rushton (1978) carried out a study to investigate whether people living in small towns would be more helpful than people living in a large city. Individuals living in a number of different-sized locations were asked questions, such as, 'Do you have change for the telephone?' or 'Can you tell me the time?' The degree of helpfulness was correlated with the size of the location. Results showed that people in the suburbs or small towns were more likely to be helpful than were people in large cities. This indicated that there was a negative correlation between the size of the town and the helpfulness of the people. The larger the town, the less helpful the people were.

Strengths and Weaknesses of Correlation

Strengths

1. *Detecting relationships.* Correlation is valuable in that it is possible to identify the direction and strength of the relationship between two (or more) variables. An added advantage is that it allows an investigator to measure relationships between naturally occurring variables without manipulating or controlling them.
2. *Correlation and prediction.* Another important use of correlation is that, if we know there is a high correlation between two variables, it allows us (cautiously) to predict the probable value of one variable if we know the value of the other. For example, if research showed that there was a high negative correlation between the amount of TV watched and end-of-term grades, you would predict that the 'compulsive' viewer would not get a very good grade. However you would not be able to say that TV viewing *caused* the low grades. Both TV viewing and low grades could be affected by a third variable, such as low ability or lack of interest in a subject. (See 'Correlation and cause' below.)

With perfect relationships, predictions can be made with absolute certainty. With imperfect relationships, you may make a guess, but how good that guess is will depend upon the degree of correlation. The closer it is to 1, the more confidence you can have in the accuracy of your guess.

3. *Correlation to assess the independence of concepts.* Correlation is valuable in that it is possible to use it to assess whether the ideas we are examining are distinct and separate or whether they are different facets of the same thing. For instance, Witkin *et al.* (1962) investigated the cognitive style defined as field independence, the ability to analyse a problem distinct from its context. He claimed that field independence should be viewed as a human characteristic that was quite separate from intelligence. In support of this claim he reported a correlational analysis of children's scores on verbal and some performance components of the Wechsler Intelligence Scales with their score on a measure of field independence. The analysis showed no significant relationship between the two measures, suggesting that they were not measuring the same thing. Other researchers, however, have produced correlational evidence which revealed a high positive correlation between the two tests, suggesting that the two tests may be measuring some of the same characteristics.

Weaknesses

1. *Correlation and cause.* It is vital to understand that correlation does not imply that one variable has caused the other. There may be several variables that are interrelated and it is difficult to know whether or not the two which have been chosen for comparison are related by cause and effect. In Hill *et al.*'s study above, for instance, the success of the participants' relationships might just as easily be the result of the amount of time they were able to spend together as a result of their similarity to each other.

2. *Extrapolation.* There is a temptation to extrapolate from the findings of a correlational study. We must keep within the limits of the data which have been collected. If a study showed that there was a high correlation between the amount of homework a group of children did each evening and their success in examinations – the homework varying between, say, half an hour and three hours, and their exam success varying between

one and six GCSE passes at Grade A – it would not be justified to suggest that the children might achieve ten passes at Grade A if they each did five hours a night homework.

Self-assessment Questions

1. Describe briefly what is meant by correlation coefficients of + 1.0, − 1.0 and zero.
2. Describe how a correlation may help assess factors as being the same rather than separate and different.
3. Why can you not infer cause from correlation?

SECTION V   PSYCHOMETRICS

The study of psychometrics involves the development and administration of tests designed to measure psychological attributes such as intelligence, creativity, personality and the like. It is obviously useful to be able to measure human attributes in order to predict a little more accurately how individuals are likely to behave in the future. This can affect such things as selection for jobs and the diagnosis of problems. The range of psychological tests is now enormous and institutions such as the National Foundation for Educational Research were formed specifically for the purpose of test development. Every trait and ability of humans is seen by the proponents of psychometry to be measurable. Some attributes are much more amenable than others to testing. The measurement of intelligence in various forms has produced many tests, including some, such as the Stanford Binet test of intelligence, that have continued to be used for decades. On the other hand, tests of creativity produced by Guilford and others in the 1950s and 1960s have not received the currency accorded to intelligence tests. This acceptability depends upon criteria such as **reliability**, **validity** and **standardisation**.

Reliability

The concept of reliability implies that the test will perform consistently, always provided that what it is measuring remains the same. There are interrelated concepts involved here.

Consistency Over Time

It is clearly necessary, if we are to have confidence in a test, for it to measure consistently over a period of time. Where a group of participants is retested after the lapse of, say, a month, a reliable test would need to produce very similar results: there would need to be a high correlation between individuals' scores on the test and their scores on the retest. This is known as **test–retest reliability**.

Sometimes it is not really feasible to retest participants using the identical test: there might be too much learning resulting from the first test. In that case an alternative parallel form of the test could be used. Eysenck and Eysenck (1964) produced two parallel forms of their Personality Inventory for this reason.

Internal Consistency

It is also necessary to ensure that the test is consistent in content. It would not be useful to have a test, some parts of which produced results markedly different from others. Accordingly it is common to test for this internal consistency by means of a split-half test, which involves correlating the scores obtained on odd-numbered items against those on even-numbered ones. Again a high correlation would be expected – perhaps $+ 0.8$ or $+ 0.9$.

Validity

For a test to be valid it needs to be shown that it tests what it sets out to test. For example, if an individual sets out to test the historical knowledge of a group of students and then, when coming to mark the test, takes off marks for spelling mistakes, that test is likely not to be valid as it is testing spelling and not just history.

The type of validity which needs to be tested depends upon the purpose of the test. It may be necessary to test **predictive validity**, **face validity**, **content validity**, **concurrent validity** or **construct validity**.

Predictive Validity

Sometimes tests are used to predict how well students are likely to perform on a course. The **predictive validity** might be tested by correlating the test scores before the course with some measure of success on the course, perhaps examination results. If there is a high positive correlation, the test can be used on incoming students as a measure of their likely success on the course.

Face Validity

A test also needs to look as though it is testing what it aims to test. A test of typing skill would have **face validity** for secretaries but not for firefighters.

Content Validity

This implies that the test tests those skills required for good performance. To refer back to an earlier example, it is not necessary to be able to spell well to be a good historian, but it is an essential skill for a good secretary. A spelling test would have content validity for secretarial skills, but not for historical knowledge.

Concurrent Validity

When the results of a test on a group of participants are compared with the results of another test of the same thing and on the same group of participants there should be a very high correlation, again + 0.8 or + 0.9. This is known as **concurrent validity**. This is a useful technique for assessing the validity of a new test by comparing it with an established one.

Construct Validity

This refers to the accuracy with which a test measures the psychological construct indicated by the theory which underlies it. This is difficult to achieve, particularly where there is disagreement between testmakers about the definition of a particular construct, as is the case with intelligence. If the aim is to establish the construct validity of an intelligence test then the test ought to correlate highly with other manifestations of intelligence, such as success in school performance. This is known as **construct validity**.

Standardisation

To be of value a test needs to be **standardised**. A set of norms for the test needs to be established. To say that a child only scored 30 per cent in a mathematics test means nothing at all in itself. However, if you have established that the norm – that is, the percentages obtained by similar participants of the same age and background – is 50 per cent on this test, then you can say that your participant has not performed well on the test.

To obtain this norm it is necessary to test a large, representative sample of the group for whom the test is intended. A normal distribution may be obtained; that is to say, a symmetrical distribution where the largest number of scores cluster around the mean (the arithmetical average). Because the characteristics of this 'normal' distribution are known, comparisons can be easily made whenever the tests are used. For instance, it is known that 68.26 per cent of scores on a normal distribution fall within one **standard deviation** of the mean, 95.44 per cent fall within two standard deviations of the mean. So it can be estimated how likely it is for any score to occur.

An example might make this clearer. If the score of 30 per cent in mathematics, mentioned above, compares with a mean score of 50 per cent on the representative sample, which has a standard deviation of 10, it is two standard deviations below the mean. Because it is below the mean, we are concerned with only one-half of the distribution – the bottom 50 per cent – and so the two standard deviations below the mean contain 47.72 per cent of the scores (that is half of 95.44 per cent). The score of 30 per cent, therefore, is in the bottom two and a half per cent – not very good at all!

Standard Scores

It is a short step from here to converting scores into standard scores. An example is a z score. This has – quite arbitrarily – a mean of 0 and a standard deviation of 1, so that the score of 30 per cent mentioned above could be converted into a z score, for example, of -2 standard deviations. Another example is a quotient, which has, again arbitrarily, a mean of 100 and a standard deviation of 15. On this basis, the maths score of 30 per cent becomes a quotient of 70. This is the usual way in which intelligence tests are expressed. Figure 4.1 illustrates standardisation.

FIGURE 4.1
The Normal Curve and Standardisation

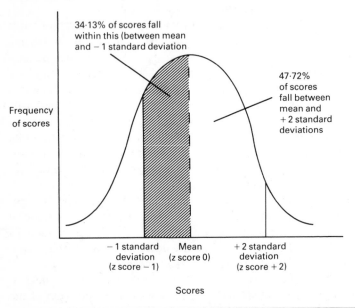

34·13% of scores fall within this (between mean and − 1 standard deviation

47·72% of scores fall between mean and + 2 standard deviations

Frequency of scores

− 1 standard deviation (z score − 1)

Mean (z score 0)

+ 2 standard deviation (z score + 2)

Scores

Strengths and Weaknesses of Psychometric Methods

Strengths

1. Psychometry is firmly based upon attempts to measure and express numerically the characteristics of behaviour in individuals. It is therefore likely to be an objective and scientific way of describing people and their behaviour.
2. The psychometric approach concentrates upon individual differences, and differences between individuals form a core on which psychology is based, and upon the description and analysis of these differences between people as a basis for the

understanding of human behaviour. This is perhaps a more valid approach to the understanding of behaviour than one which isolates particular behaviours and attempts to explain them.

Weaknesses

1. *The problem of labelling.* The assumption is made by some proponents of psychometrics that characteristics to be measured are fixed and invariant, both in relation to time, and also in relation to circumstance or situation. Let us take, for example, the measurement of personality traits. An individual participant may be measured as being introverted on a well established and validated test of personality. While that may be true at that time, in six months that individual might have changed considerably, perhaps because of a new job, providing increased confidence. Similarly the assumption is made that the measurement made is not situation-specific. The individual concerned may be shy and introverted in the formal company of the workplace, but at home may be much more extravert and outgoing.

   There is also the chance that the labelling of an individual as possessing a particular trait – say dominance – will tend to encourage conformity to that trait, as was seen when we were discussing expectancy.

2. *Lack of flexibility.* The psychometric approach implies a nomothetic view of people; that is to say, a view that people are capable of being classified and measured. The opposing view to this would argue that humans are essentially individuals and not susceptible to classification, an **idiographic** view. This dichotomy is discussed in Chapter 3.

3. *Measurement and concepts.* The view is frequently taken that the very fact that something is measured makes it exist as a concept. It has been said that 'intelligence is what intelligence tests measure'. The concept of intelligence might not have existed at all if Binet had not set out to measure it. Intelligence came to be defined in terms of test performance rather than as an entity in itself.

Self-assessment Questions

1. What are the main aims of those psychologists who make use of psychometric methods?
2. Write down a brief explanation of what is meant by: reliability, validity, standardisation.
3. List two weaknesses of the psychometric method.

FURTHER READING

F. Clegg, *Simple Statistics – A Course Book for the Social Sciences* (Cambridge: Cambridge University Press, 1982).

H. Coolican, *Research Methods and Statistics in Psychology* (London: Hodder & Stoughton, 1990).

S. Miller, *Experimental Design and Statistics* (London: Methuen, 1984).

C. Robson, *Experiment Design and Statistics in Psychology*, 2nd edn (Harmondsworth: Penguin, 1984).

HIM? HE'S THE EDUCATIONAL PSYCHOLOGIST.

What Do Psychologists Do? 5

At the end of this chapter you should be able to:

1. identify the content of the main fields of pure research in psychology;
2. describe some of the main areas of applied research;
3. show how psychological concepts have been applied to therapy; and
4. identify some of the career openings for psychologists.

Introduction

Psychology is not quite the same as other subjects in that it is not only a subject but also a profession. Its professional body, The British Psychological Society (BPS), offers graduate membership to those who have a degree with sufficient psychological content, and regulates the way in which psychologists behave in terms of such things as ethics, a topic dealt with more fully in Chapter 6. What this chapter will attempt to do is to give a picture of the varied outlets for those with qualifications in psychology. In most instances, this means a degree. While GCSE or GCE A or AS level Psychology have value as an interesting subject to study, it is only an introduction, and use of psychology depends on further study and training.

The fields which will be dealt with here fall into the following broad categories: (1) pure psychological research; (2) applied psychology: (a) non-therapeutic – either research into the practical uses of psychological knowledge or the application of this knowledge in the field; and (b) therapeutic – the use of psychological knowledge and skill in treatment of abnormal conditions.

SECTION I   PURE RESEARCH

Pure research into psychology is carried on mainly by University and Polytechnic Departments of Psychology following the interests of the members of staff engaged in it. It aims to extend knowledge and it does not, in the short term at least, aim at changing the way in which people behave, but rather at understanding why they behave as they do. Psychologists engaged in pure research start from what has been found out already or from questioning existing theories and knowledge. Then, making use of the scientific method (described in Chapter 6), they set up hypotheses and test them. For example, in the field of research into memory, Sperling (1960) had established the existence of what was termed a 'Visual Information Store' – a brief prolongation of a visual stimulus to enable it to be processed and passed to the short-term memory store. Treisman (1964), using Sperling's work as a basis, attempted to establish the existence of an 'Echoic Store', the equivalent within the hearing modality of Sperling's Visual Information Store.

The fields of study covered in this kind of basic pure research are illustrated in Figure 5.1 below:

There follows a brief description of the work carried out in each of these fields of study to give an idea of the scope of psychology, but even this is not exhaustive. The study of psychology includes anything that humans (or animals) do.

Cognitive Psychology

Cognitive psychology is a central discipline of psychology. It is concerned with the way in which the nervous system processes information. Under the influence of the behaviourists (see Chapters 1 and 2) this area once tended to be neglected in favour of the study of stimulus (what went into the mind) and response (the

FIGURE 5.1
Areas of Pure Research

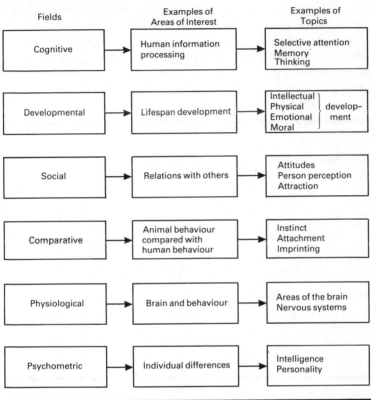

behaviour which resulted). The way information was processed was thought to be inaccessible and so was ignored.

A typical method of working in the field of cognitive psychology has been to set up a hypothetical model of what might be happening in the nervous system as information is processed and then testing the model through empirical research (see Chapter 2, Section IV).

We might take as an example some work done on the topic of attention; that is, how the mind selects some information to process out of the mass which is presented to it. A model of the way this selection occurs was set up by (amongst others) Broadbent (1958) which suggested that the available capacity of the mind to deal with information was limited and that there needed to be a filter mechanism of some kind to select what most immediately needed to be dealt with (see Figure 5.2). The model arose from observations made by Colin Cherry and others about the way in which individuals were able to focus upon one conversation in a crowded party, paying little attention to everything else that was going on.

FIGURE 5.2
Broadbent's Filter Model of Selective Attention

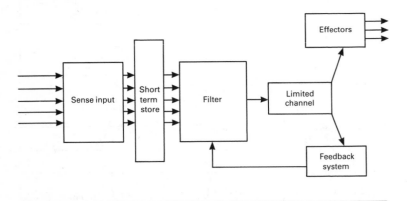

What Broadbent was attempting to do in developing this model was to create a framework, based on observations already made, for an explanation of the stages of processing which are carried on in the brain – which after all is not accessible to direct observation. The framework can then be supported, refuted or modified as a result of data acquired through experiment.

In Broadbent's case this experimental evidence included 'split-span' experiments. In these, participants were presented through earphones with a series of digits to recall sent alternately to the left and right ears. He found that the participants would recall first all the digits presented to one ear, then all presented to the other: for example, 567821 might be presented:

left	*right*
5	6
7	8
2	1

Participants would recall 572 then 681. When they were asked to recall the pairs, 56:78:21, recall was only 20 per cent. He concluded that a filter system, such as he had hypothesised, had filtered out all the input to one ear before it allowed through to processing the input from the other ear. Other researchers, such as Treisman, concluded that Broadbent's model did not account adequately for all the observed data, and so modified the model to include an attenuating unit which weakens but does not eliminate entirely the message which is not being attended to immediately. In this way understanding of cognitive processes is advanced.

Cognitive Science

With the growth of the study of **artificial intelligence (AI)** and the increasing use of computers in the modelling of cognitive processes, there has been a growing demand for Cognitive Science to be recognised as a separate discipline. Brown (1990) has suggested that there are three alternative views regarding this development:

1. The 'new-discipline' model of cognitive science. This view suggests that mental states can be replicated and studied on computers. Cognitive science is therefore a new discipline with its own subject matter (intelligent systems, both natural and artificial) and its own vocabulary.
2. The 'umbrella' view of computer science. This second view emphasises the interdisciplinary nature of the new field of cognitive science. It is not a new and separate discipline but provides a whole range of new tools for the study of cognitive processes.
3. **Eco-cognitivism**. This view involves a rejection of the notion that it may be possible to study and replicate mental states independently of the ecology in which they occur; that is to say, causes and effects in the real world. There are two broad themes within this ecological view: (a) a denial that structured mental representation in isolation is as important as the cogni-

tivists maintain; and (b) an insistence that any representation of mental process must have meaning 'in the world' rather than just 'in the head'.

Developmental Psychology

Developmental psychology is concerned with the way in which humans develop and change throughout their lifespan, though perhaps the focus has been particularly upon the development of children. A variety of methods have been used: observation, experiment and case study in particular. This can be illustrated by looking at the research of Bower (1965) into the development of perception. He aimed to show that babies aged between 40 and 60 days were able to perceive size constancy; that is, they had the ability to perceive an object as the same size no matter from what distance it is viewed. The child was trained by means of a peek-a-boo game to respond by turning its head towards a cube which was of two different sizes and at two different distances from the child. There were four conditions:

1. the control condition to which the child had been trained – a 30 cm cube at 1 metre,
2. 30 cm at 3 metres,
3. 90 cm at 1 metre,
4. 90 cm at 3 metres.

Bower predicted that, if the child had not achieved size constancy, there would be the same response of head turning to condition 4 as to the original control condition, since the image received by the eye would be the same for both. If, on the other hand, the child had achieved size constancy there would be a response to 2 only (the original cube placed further away). The results appeared to show that the children tested had achieved size constancy.

The above research uses **experimental method**. An example of the use of **observation** in developmental psychology might be the work of Sylva *et al.* (1980) investigating play in nursery classes in Oxfordshire (referred to in Chapter 4, Section II). The researchers divided play into high-, medium- and low-yield activities – high-yield activities being such things as building, drawing and doing puzzles; medium-yield activities including pretend play and play with sand or dough; and low-yield activities including unstructured social playing and rough and tumble. It was suggested that the high-yield activities were more cognitively useful than the medium- and low-yield activities.

Case study has also been extensively used in developmental psychology, by such people as Piaget in his earlier investigation of intellectual development and by Melanie Klein in her studies of emotional development. Developmental psychology does not of course confine itself to childhood. Neugarten (1973, 1977) conducted studies into the way in which individuals approach the last years of their life, testing an earlier theory proposed by Cumming and Henry (1961) which became known as 'disengagement theory'. It suggests that, as individuals approach the last years of life, they progressively withdraw from social contacts and activities, become less concerned with the problems of the outside world, separating themselves from emotional attachments with other people. Neugarten suggested that, while this disengagement undoubtedly occurs, friendships and social relationships remain important and may compensate for losses during old age. This finding has been supported by Tesch (1983).

Social Psychology

Social psychologists are concerned to investigate the effects upon individuals' behaviour of belonging to a group or being involved with other people. Methods include both experimental observational and survey methods. Baron-Cohen (1988), for example, explained the phenomenon of autism as an impairment of the ability to understand the thoughts and feelings of others. Baron-Cohen, Leslie and Frith (1985) conducted an experiment to test this explanation.

A child is seated at a table on which there are two dolls (named Anne and Sally) and two boxes (one square, the other round). A marble is hidden under one box 'by' Anne while Sally looks on. Sally then 'leaves the room' and the marble is re-hidden under the other box. Sally then 'returns' and the child is asked three questions:

1. Where will Sally look for her marble? (Belief question)
2. Where is the marble really? (Reality question)

3. Where was the marble in the beginning? (Memory question)

The 20 autistic children tested had an average mental age of 9 years and 3 months (their average chronological age was 11 years 11 months). Also tested were 14 Down's syndrome children (average age 10 years and 11 months) and 27 normal children (average age 4 years and 5 months).

All the children answered the reality and memory questions correctly and 86 per cent of Down's syndrome and 85 per cent of normal children answered the belief question correctly, but only 20 per cent of the autistic children did so. They pointed to the marble's current location rather than where it was originally hidden. Autistic children tend to fail on the belief question because they lack the capacity to imagine the beliefs of others.

Examples of studies using survey methods might include that of Joy, Kimball and Zabrack (1977) who studied the incidence of aggression in a small Canadian community before and after the introduction of television into the town. Observation, both participative and non-participative, was used by Corsaro (1985) to examine friendships made among nursery school children. He used one-way mirrors and videotapes as well as joining in with the children's activities. The results stressed the importance of the social context within which children operate and the way children's concepts about friendship emerge in response to the demands of everyday situations.

Comparative Psychology

Comparative psychologists study the behaviour of animals and make comparisons with human behaviour. Animals are less complex than humans: accordingly variables are easier to control. Also it is possible to use animals in a way which would not be ethically possible with human participants. The question of the use of animals in research is discussed more fully in Chapter 6.

Lea (1984) suggests that there are three main approaches to comparative psychology.

Comparative Ethology

This is the oldest and best known of these approaches, exemplified in the work of Lorenz and Tinbergen, who suggested that be-haviour might be studied in the same way as other aspects of life. Just as the biological forms of animals which belong to related groups of species will tend to be similar, so their behaviour is also likely to be similar. For example, Leyhausen (1973), investigating drives, noted that there is a build-up of drive energy which may be released by appropriate behaviour: hunger drive is released by eating, for instance. Leyhausen used cats' hunting behaviour by way of illustration. While a well-fed cat will not hunt much, in a glut of mice, when a cat has caught several without having to stalk them, it will start stalking more distant mice. It seems that the glut of mice has not 'released' built-up stalking behaviour. Ethologists concluded that there were 'action-specific energies'. Each fixed action pattern seems to have its own specifically related drive.

Social Ethology

This represents the way in which biologists study societies. They start from the social environment of animals. In 1976, E.O. Wilson published *Sociobiology* and in 1977 Richard Dawkins published *The Selfish Gene*. They treated animal societies as biological entities. Of every piece of behaviour the question is asked whether the gene which produced that behaviour could survive in evolu-tionary terms. An important aspect of animals' environments, though, is other members of the species which form their social group.

Behavioural Ecology

Behavioural ecologists are also interested in behaviour, but from the point of view which considers how certain behaviour affects the distribution of a species. There has been interest, for example, in the way in which animals learn where to forage. Krebs, Kacelnik and Taylor (1978) arranged an experiment in which great tits could obtain food by hopping onto either of two perches, which provided them with different probabilities of obtaining food. At first they sampled both perches, but in the end hopped consistently onto the one which was more likely to yield food, a result which could have been predicted under Krebs *et al.*'s' **optimal foraging theory**.

Physiological Psychology

The approach of physiological psychologists is to look for explanations of behaviour in the physiological structures of humans and animals. Animals are frequently used for the reasons described above, and so there are close links with comparative psychology. In particular, study is concentrated upon the brain and the nervous system, as being most influential in determining behaviour, though the endocrine system is also important. Methods of study include clinical examination of patients who have behavioural abnormality, usually as a result of disease or trauma; in the study of memory for instance, Shallice and Warrington (1977) showed that some patients with damage to the left parietal cortex had problems with short-term memory. Their digit spans were reduced to one or two items instead of the normal seven.

Measurement of physiological phenomena such as heart rate, blood pressure, sweating, galvanic skin response (GSR), in relation to strong emotion is another example; Sternbach (1962) showed children the film *Bambi* and measured the physiological changes that occurred in them as they watched the saddest, · scariest, happiest and funniest parts of the film. An increase in GSR was noted in the saddest parts, while the happiest scenes were accompanied by gastric contraction.

Electroencephalography (EEG) has been used to record the electrical patterns of the brain in sleep research. In animals the use of **ablation** or **lesion** techniques – the removal or cutting of parts of the brain – interfering with normal brain structures and observing the resultant changes in behaviour has increased knowledge of brain function. Jouvet (1967), for example, was able to show, through making lesions in the brain stem, that an area known as the **locus coerulus** was responsible for rapid eye movement (REM) sleep. When the area was lesioned REM sleep was suppressed.

The use of **microelectrodes** to record and sometimes to stimulate particular neurons within the brain has been demonstrated by, for example, Hubel and Wiesel (1962), who were able to record the activity of particular neurons in the visual cortex on the presentation of certain stimuli.

Chemical stimulation is also used to alter the way in which transmitter substances affect neural activity in the brain. Grossman (1960), for example, found that an injection of acetylcholine into the hypothalamus resulted in drinking, while an injection of noradrenalin resulted in eating; thus he was able to show that motivation to eat and to drink was controlled by separate nerve pathways.

Psychometrics

Psychologists in the field of **psychometrics** attempt to measure attributes of human individual differences – intelligence, aptitudes, personality, attitudes – to mention only a few of the many measurements that are made. Whether this work comes strictly within the scope of pure psychology is perhaps debatable. As with many other fields there is a 'pure' element, the identification of a concept, say, creativity and the behaviours which make up the concept, and then tests are devised to measure those behaviours. Thus Guilford (1950) worked on the structure of the intellect, identified 120 different abilities and devised tests for a large proportion of them. Very often statistical procedures such as factor analysis are used to find out the degree to which it is possible to identify factors which go to make up the concept under investigation. Guilford, in studying creativity, also proposed that it involved divergent thinking, some convergent thinking, and evaluation. A battery of tests was devised for these factors and the combined results of these tests purported to be tests of 'creativity'.

The value of psychometric tests in a practical context lies in their ability to reduce the need for guesswork in the selection of individuals for particular roles. However the use of psychometric tests for the selection of children for particular forms of education, for example, the 11 plus test for selection for grammar schools has been the subject of criticism. It was felt that the concept of intelligence which underlay the selection tests was not sufficiently well understood, and that it was not a unitary or a stable attribute, as had been assumed.

Psychopathology

Psychopathology is the study of mental disorder. Here again it is not easy to separate 'pure' research into the nature of abnormalities from 'applied' research into appropriate ways of treating those with abnormalities. Essentially those engaged in 'pure' research in this area might, for example, be investigating the function of dopamine as a neurotransmitter. Applied research might involve the development of drugs which could block the action of dopamine in the case of schizophrenia, or alternatively the development of drugs which increase its availability in the case of Parkinsonism.

Self-assessment Questions

1. Why do cognitive psychologists use models?
2. What is the main thrust of those who engage in psychometric research?
3. What kind of issues do social psychologists address?

SECTION II   APPLIED RESEARCH

Non-therapeutic Applications

Applied research is carried out either in an academic environment – a university or a polytechnic – or in a work context. Typically the problem posed will be a practical one, in contrast to pure research which tends not to be so much problem-based as theory-based. The work of the Applied Psychology Unit (APU) at Cambridge University is a good example. The APU was started by Craik and Bartlett, carried on by Broadbent and Baddeley, and produced not only practical solutions to problems but also theoretical contributions to areas of knowledge such as attention, vigilance and memory. At the same time, their advice has influenced such practical outcomes as the design of decimal coinage and postal codes. Broadbent has been concerned practically with such problems as how noise affects people's ability to make decisions and attend to the task in hand. Real problems, such as the ergonomic design of pilots' cockpit control panels or systems for radar operators are dealt with.

In an academic context such as that enjoyed by the APU, problems are solved mainly through simulating them in the laboratory, for example setting up a simulation of a radar operator's workplace and then testing for the effects of such things as stress on performance.

Alternatively, applied psychology may involve action research in the workplace. **Participant observation** might be used (see Chapter 4). Warr (1978) became a member of a trade union negotiating team to gain first-hand experience of the methods used by employers and unions. This is applied social psychology.

Again it is useful to look at some examples of applied research in the fields mentioned above.

Applied Research in Cognitive Psychology

Bach-y-Rita *et al.* (1969) worked on what became known as 'blind-sight'. This was the development of a tactile sensory re-placement for normal sight. The user wears a vest with a grid on which are hundreds of tiny points that touch the skin. The vest is connected to a black and white camera; light and dark messages are gathered by the camera and translated into vibrations on the points on the vest. With this equipment blind people have been able to find things in a room quickly, read meters and even read an oscilloscope.

Applied Research in Developmental Psychology

The Cockcroft committee was set up to enquire into the question of why there seemed to be so many problems associated with the learning of mathematics in schools (DES, 1982). The committee received evidence of research on learning and teaching mathema-tics which was reviewed by Bell *et al.* (1983). They concluded that mathematics was hard to learn because it tended to deal with abstract relationships. This concentration on abstracts has been highlighted by the growth in the use of calculators to perform the basic symbol manipulations which had at one time been seen as the core of mathematics as learnt in school. If you could manipulate the right symbols in the right order you could get the answer right, whether or not you had any understanding of the underlying concepts. With the use of calculators the focus began to be placed on developing an understanding of the concepts, rather than just on symbol manipulation, and it has been this that has proved difficult for many children.

Piaget showed that abstract concepts were difficult to acquire. The formal operations stage of development was the point at which children began to be able to deal with abstracts. For most children this was at about age 11 and, for some, much later than this. In fact Shayer and Wylam (1978) claim that only about 20 per cent of British children reach the formal operational stage by age 16. Assuming, therefore, that most of the children in secondary schools are still at the concrete operational stage, more attention should be paid to the level of thought required in working through textbooks in mathematics, which should themselves be directed more towards concrete operations. The solution is to use apparatus to build bridges between concrete and abstract thought and to encourage children to develop mathematical thought through language.

Applied Research in Social Psychology

Perhaps the most important application of social psychology lies in the field of **organisational psychology**. Blackler and Brown (1980) reported revolutionary changes in the field of job-design in the Volvo plant in Sweden. Because of high customer demand there was a need to increase production of trucks. The existing assembly lines were working at maximum capacity. A new and unconventional approach was adopted which involved a semi-autonomous team of workers assembling around a static chassis. Since the days of Henry Ford it had been thought that the static assembly of vehicles was much less efficient than moving assembly lines. With a motivated, skilled and co-operative workforce, however, it seemed that savings of something like 30 per cent could be achieved by this new method of static assembly. There was enthusiasm on the part of the workers for the new method and its potential began to be realised, so that even when demand slackened the company did not shut down the experimental unit, but continued to explore its feasibility. From a psychological standpoint it maximised the variety of work for an individual and provided learning opportunities, responsibility and involvement in the whole task. However opinion among the managers at the factory hardened against innovation and eventually, when a new plant was built in 1979, it was along more conventional lines.

One reason why this experiment did not succeed was the conservatism of senior managers. It had become a feature of the experimental static plant that, once the quota for the day had been achieved, workers had been allowed some relaxation at their work station. Management, however, reacted to this by increasing work quotas, and this had a demoralising effect. Loss of managerial control in the new method was considered to be an insuperable obstacle in the way of establishing what had at first been shown to be a more effective method of work.

Applications of Comparative Psychology

It cannot be said that there is strictly applied research in the field of **comparative psychology**. A researcher does not deliberately set out to use psychological research to solve a particular problem, as in the example above of research into the learning of mathematics. It is, however, true that much has been learned about human behaviour from the studies of animals conducted by **ethologists**. For example, **displacement** activities have been much researched by ethologists where there is a drive-conflict situation. Animals will engage in totally unrelated activity in the stress of conflict between wanting to do and being afraid of doing something. A cock zebra finch in conflict between approaching a hen and flying away from her may wipe his beak violently on the perch. A human teenager waiting for a first date may indulge in one of a number of displacement activities – chewing nails, adjusting make-up, straightening a tie or smoothing a skirt. But this is not applied psychology. It is the application of pure psychology in explanation of behaviour.

Section II of Chapter 6 contains several examples of the application of comparative psychology. Lea (1984) identifies four ways of applying the results of studying animal behaviour.

1. Ethology provides insights which are of benefit in such situations as the interaction of humans with animals on farms, zoos and wildlife reserves and the keeping of pets by individuals. In particular, the mating behaviour of endangered species can be singled out. It is necessary when natural habitats are destroyed to induce species to breed in captivity. Knowledge of normal mating procedures enables us to simulate the conditions which might enable them to reproduce.
2. In their study of animals ethologists employ carefully planned observational techniques. These methods have been adapted

and used for the study of humans. This **human ethology** has been particularly successful in the study of babies and young children. Among many examples described by Schaffer (1977) there is a detailed description of 'states' – classified by Prechtl and Beintema (1964) – of babies ranging from 'deep regular sleep' (state 1) to 'crying' (state 5). These states were seen as cyclical. Not only is the baby stirred into action by outside stimulation but internal forces regulate much of a baby's behaviour.

3. Sometimes the ideas and concepts of ethology may be incorporated into psychological theory. Hediger (1951) in his analysis of the behaviour of zoo animals developed the concept of 'individual distance', the space which individuals of the same species always seem to try to keep between each other. This has been adopted into the social psychology of humans as the concept of **personal space**.

4. Most questionably, results from ethological studies have been extrapolated into human study. Desmond Morris (1978) for instance has attempted this kind of extrapolation, concentrating particularly upon non-verbal communication.

Applied Psychometrics

Psychometric research has been largely applied in that tests of individuals' characteristics have been designed, not so much with the pure goal of better understanding the differences between people, as for the practical object of placing people in suitable employment or – to stand that on its head – to find suitable employees to fill a vacancy. Trainability testing (Robertson and Downs, 1979) has been developed in recent years. This is a form of testing where applicants are given a period of training in the skills they are required to learn and then systematically observed and rated as they attempt to carry out the task. It is job-specific and requires no prior knowledge or experience on the part of the candidate. Trainability tests have been shown to be valuable in semi-skilled manual tasks, and also in discovering management potential.

Therapeutic Applications

Different kinds of therapy spring from the main approaches to psychology: behaviourist, psychoanalytic, cognitive and humanistic.

Behaviour Modification

The technique of **behaviour modification** (see Chapter 2, Section III) has been used quite extensively in the treatment of abnormal behaviour, particularly in children. In essence, it amounts to the application of conditioning procedures, especially **operant conditioning**, to change the behaviour of those treated. It has been used, for example, to treat people with mental handicaps so that they exhibit behaviour which is more acceptable to the group with whom they are associated. The procedure is to isolate desired behaviour, which is then systematically reinforced, while reinforcement is withheld from undesirable behaviour. Research into the treatment by this means of agoraphobia (fear of leaving a safe and secure place) has resulted in increased effectiveness of treatment and reduction of therapist time.

Psychoanalytic Therapy

Psychoanalytic therapy arises from the practices of Freud and his followers (see Chapter 2, Section II), and is based upon the uncovering of problems concealed in the unconscious mind, perhaps from childhood, and with their revelation, coming to terms with problems currently exhibited. Interest is beginning to build up in Britain in this area of research with the establishment of a Psychoanalysis Unit in the University of London and of research into the process of psychotherapy in the Social and Applied Psychology Unit at Sheffield University. An example might be the use of play therapy by Melanie Klein (see Chapter 2) and her associates (Klein, 1959). Klein provided carefully chosen toys and play materials for children referred to her and allowed them freedom to play as they wished under her observation. She sat or knelt with individual children as they played and interpreted their behaviour in psychoanalytic terms; that is to say, she considered how the behaviour observed might have a symbolic relationship with some past experience which had become a part of the unconscious and was affecting the child's personality.

Cognitive Therapy

Cognitive therapy is being increasingly used by clinical psychologists in the treatment of depression and other disorders. Its initial effectiveness has been shown to compare favourably with the use of medication. Cognitive therapy is used on the assumption that a person suffering from depression tends to have a memory system biased towards negative material, and these negative memories contribute to the maintenance of the depressed mood. The aim of cognitive therapy is to replace these negative memories with more positive ones. Cognitive psychology has also been used in the treatment of occupational stress, a condition which is becoming increasingly common. Treatment with tranquillising drugs is common, but psychological therapies aim to help patients to see their world differently and to accept personal responsibility for their own lives. It is into this category of therapy that the rapidly increasing role of counselling may be placed.

Therapy Based Upon Humanistic Psychology

Client-centred therapy such as that offered by centres whose work is based on that of Carl Rogers (See Chapter 2, Section V) is increasingly being used as an alternative to other treatments. The aim is to help clients to come to terms with themselves. By means of individual therapy, group or family therapy sessions, a more realistic evaluation of an individual's self-concept emerges which is closer to a conception of the person's ideal self. The process is one of non-intervention by the therapist whose role is to encourage clients to talk about themselves or to each other and who is trained in counselling techniques designed to help people find their own solution to problems.

One of the difficulties in the field of psychotherapy is that at present it is open to anyone to set up as a psychotherapist without necessarily having undergone any training or education in psychology. The whole situation should become more stable and coherent now that the British Psychological Society has introduced a register of chartered psychologists.

Self-assessment Questions

1. What contributions did the Applied Psychology Unit at Cambridge make to the solution of practical problems?
2. Describe one area of applied research in developmental or educational psychology.
3. How has applied social psychology been used in an industrial context?
4. List four ways in which comparative psychology has been applied in practical situations.
5. Describe some therapeutic applications of psychology.

SECTION III   CAREER OPENINGS FOR PSYCHOLOGISTS

The above sections will have given some indication of the kind of work done by psychologists. It is worth emphasising that psychology is a graduate profession and the openings described below assume the possession of a degree in psychology, or one that is recognised by the British Psychological Society.

Occupational Psychology

There are many who hold psychological qualifications employed in industry and the public service, in particular the Civil Service and HM Forces. The kind of work they do has already been alluded to. As employees are selected for employment the psychologist has a role in their selection and in their training. The development of aptitude tests for particular jobs is part of their function, as is the assessment of their performance within their employment. Personnel management too is an area heavily dependent upon psychological skills and postgraduate courses leading to membership of the Institute of Personnel Management will inevitably have a high psychological content. The National Institute of Industrial Psychology runs training courses and validates tests of aptitude in this field of occupational psychology.

Occupational health is another area in which psychologists in the occupational field are becoming involved. This started about ten years ago as a result of growing concern for occupational stress. It now embraces all aspects of employee health care.

Another area which has received attention from occupational psychologists is that of the interface between humans and computers. Factories, hospitals and small businesses are increasingly using micros, word processors and so on and the relationship between person and machine is becoming important for productivity, health, career development and work roles. There has been an overwhelming interest in applied research in this field. The issues include: (1) negative health consequences; (2) improvement of career prospects; and (3) clarification of role relationships, which become increasingly confusing with the growth of the use of micros. This has led to a new Inter-Research Council (the Economic and Social Research Council together with the Medical Research Council) initiative in the field of human–computer interaction which will receive funding for both research and training and will have a major psychological component.

A further area of research among occupational psychologists has been the question of minorities at work – especially women and ethnic groups. Research is being carried out into the way in which women are treated in industry, for example their career paths, their health and the impact of their dual roles in families where both partners have careers. While this research has led to growing demands for change in the legislative field, little has yet been done and so it is likely that research into women in the workplace will grow.

In the case of ethnic groups at work the situation is not good. Little systematic research has been done into what is becoming an increasingly difficult problem area in Britain. Areas to be tackled include: **career development**, **stress**, **co-worker relationships** and **discrimination**.

There is also research into cognitive areas specific to **occupational psychology**. In particular, **performance appraisal** has become increasingly important and efforts are beginning to be made to apply psychological theory to appraisal at work.

The enormous change which is happening in Britain, industrially and socially, has also led to the need for research into the way in which people can plan and cope with organisational change in the work situation. Occupational psychologists are beginning to make a real contribution in this area.

Clinical Psychology

Clinical psychology is concerned with the application of psychology to problems of health and illness. Clinical psychologists work mainly with psychiatrists in a hospital context. There is need for a rapid expansion in the number of clinical psychologists, but funding for sufficient training courses for the ample supply of suitably qualified applicants is presently inadequate. The route into this area of work is through a degree in psychology followed by a post-graduate qualification in clinical psychology. Most clinical psychologists are employed by Health Authorities, where their role is to work with psychiatrists in the treatment of patients suffering from psychological disorders. However an increasing number are now working with children and adolescents rather than adults. They also work with the mentally handicapped, the elderly and those who have neuropsychological problems.

Clinical psychologists are also engaged in research into psychological treatment in behavioural therapy, cognitive therapy and in the application of psychological treatment to medical disorders.

Research into Behavioural Therapy

An example might be research into the treatment of agoraphobia by 'in vivo' exposure or the use of behaviour modification to modify the behaviour of those with mental handicaps, such as autism.

Research into Psychological Treatments for Medical Conditions

There is strong evidence now for the effectiveness of psychological therapy for the treatment of hypertension. Asthma, epilepsy and chronic pain have also been subjects of encouraging research. Cognitive retraining and rehabilitation of patients with neurological handicap has also received attention and this has contributed in turn to an understanding of human brain function. There has been an extension of treatment by clinical psychologists to groups of patients not treated by them hitherto. AIDS and sexual abuse of children are two areas that might be mentioned.

Research into the nature of psychological dysfunction has been closely allied with that into treatment of abnormality. For example, there has been research into cognitive and attentional dysfunctions in cases of schizophrenia and emotional disorders. Social psychology has contributed to an understanding of the role of life events and of social support in the etiology of emotional problems. Physiological psychology has contributed to an understanding of the behavioural effects of Alzheimer's disease.

All the above indicate a rapid growth in the use of psychological expertise in clinical treatments, and this has not been matched by growth in facilities for training, so that it is becoming difficult to enter this field. Many individuals gain experience in poorly paid work in hospitals to gain appropriate experience before applying for training.

Psychodynamic Psychology

Essentially this is the psychology of unconscious mental processes, as distinct from cognitive psychology which deals with conscious processes. This has yet to be taken seriously by some professional psychologists in the mainstream of British psychology, which has meant that entry into this field has been largely unregulated and it is not easy to say that there is a clear career path.

Educational Psychology

The psychology of education has always been a central concern. There has been much theorising and empirical work carried out in this area. The Schools Psychological Service has had an impact within as well as beyond the classroom.

Someone aspiring to join the Schools Psychological Service will need, first, a good degree in psychology, and then a postgraduate teaching qualification (PGCE). Thereafter some practical experience in teaching in schools will be followed by a specific qualification in Educational Psychology before a person may apply for appointment as a member of the Schools Psychological Service of a Local Education Authority.

Despite the relevance of psychology to the training of teachers there has been a reduction in recent years of psychological content in teacher training courses and even a suggestion by government that psychology was not an appropriate discipline for aspiring members of the teaching profession. This has obviously caused problems for the recruitment and training of educational psychologists to work in the Schools Psychological Service. The educational psychologist's role has been to provide assessment and guidance for children referred to them by schools because their behaviour or progress has caused anxiety, and this role is, if anything, more necessary now than in the past.

Paradoxically the changes brought about within education by the same government have led to a resurgence of interest in both the psychology of education and in educational psychology. For instance, there has been increased interest, with the introduction of the National Curriculum, in **criterion-referenced testing, normative development** and **formative assessment**. Work in both academic and professional psychology in the field of education has been the catalyst for this developing interest in and understanding of the educational process.

Criminological and Legal Psychology

Legal psychology might involve therapeutic work with individuals or with groups of offenders. This kind of work aims at understanding and treating behaviour problems in those who have come into conflict with the law. Psychologists in this field may be involved with the organisation and evaluation of custodial regimes, clinical work with individuals after they leave the courts, or in the administration of the judicial system. They may work in prisons or in other secure establishments – detention centres or Regional Secure Units. They may be involved in doing research into the psychological processes that underlie certain offences, such as sexual offences or aggression. They may also be members of the police force.

It is possible to identify four areas of work within this field:

1. *Clinical and rehabilitative work*. This involves attempting to establish the causes of anti-social or aggressive behaviour in order to improve it through treatment.
2. *Administration*. Secure institutions are likely to employ psychologists to be involved, initially, in the planning of the units and in operational policy within the unit – allocation of resources and design of the accommodation for instance. Psychologists

are likely to sit on Home Office and Department of Health committees concerned with the future planning of special hospitals.

3. *Court work*. Criminological and legal psychologists may be involved in both criminal and civil court cases. In a civil case, this might involve using psychometric or behavioural tests to help assess the impairment of an individual's functioning following an accident. In a criminal case a psychologist might be asked to see an individual charged with a petty offence such as shoplifting and perhaps establish what the intention of the offender was. This might influence judgement and sentence.

4. *Prison service work*. A psychologist might also work in the environment of a prison. Work might include helping prison officers understand the factors which produce a build-up of tension in the prison, leading to outbreaks of violence. Teaching aspects of criminology or advising on hostage taking are also aspects of a psychologist's work with prison staff. With inmates, social skills training is important. Basically psychologists will enter the service with a good degree in psychology and may take additional qualifications such as a Master's degree in criminology. Those who work in the Secure Hospitals would expect to qualify as clinical psychologists.

Self-assessment Questions

1. List those areas of work where psychologists are likely to be found.
2. What kind of work would you expect an occupational psychologist to do?
3. What are some of the functions of clinical psychologists?

FURTHER READING

B. Ball, *Manage your own career* (Leicester: BPS Books, 1989).

British Psychological Society, *How about Psychology: A guide to courses and careers* (Leicester: BPS Books, 1986).

British Psychological Society, *Career Choices in Psychology* (Leicester: BPS Books, 1988).

British Psychological Society, *BPS Careers Pack* (Leicester: BPS Books, 1989a).

British Psychological Society, *Putting Psychology to Work* (Leicester: BPS Books, 1989b).

A.J. Chapman and A. Gale, *Psychology and People: a Tutorial Text* (Leicester: BPS/Macmillan, 1982).

I SAY, TREATED HUMANELY, IT'S PERFECTLY ETHICAL TO STUDY THEM.

Psychology and Scientific Method 6

At the end of this chapter you should be able to:

1. explain what is meant by 'scientific method';
2. discuss critically the use of scientific method in psychology;
3. discuss the use of animals in psychological research; and
4. discuss the ethical issues involved in the use of human participants in psychology

INTRODUCTION

When asked the question 'What is science?' many lay people would respond with examples of the life or physical sciences such as biology, chemistry and physics. Psychology would be unlikely to be included. They would be surprised to learn that psychology shares many of the characteristics of the natural sciences. They might argue that the subject matter does not qualify as scientific and that psychologists do not collect information in a scientific way or have scientific theories. The purpose of this chapter is to show that psychologists do adopt a scientific approach and are justified in defining psychology as the scientific study of behaviour (see Chapter 1). It is also important to evaluate this approach for its appropriateness and to highlight particular problems, such as the use of animals in research and the ethical issues which surround the use of human participants in the study of psychology.

Routes to Knowledge

The scientific method is just one way of gathering knowledge. Peirce (1951) describes a number of other ways of gaining knowledge about the world:

1. The **method of tenacity**. Tenacious believers, by frequent repetition, convince themselves of the truth of what they want to believe. They may also reinterpret information to suit their beliefs. Festinger *et al.* (1956) illustrate this. Festinger infiltrated a quasi-religious group who believed themselves to be in touch with extra-terrestrial beings from the planet 'Clarion'. They were warned of the day on which the world was to end and they were expecting to be rescued by flying saucers. When the disaster did not strike, some were disillusioned and left. Others, sure that their faith had saved the world, had their commitment strengthened. Such a route to knowledge is clearly error-prone!

2. **The method of authority**. If a credible authority asserts something is true, then it is believed to be true. The Bible, parents, the television or an 'expert' may be authorities. Belief in authority as a source of knowledge is based on trust, or it may be impracticable to verify knowledge independently. Authority is not necessarily wrong but could be unreliable for one of two reasons: (1) authority's own sources may be faulty; and (2) the experts might be swayed by their own values, prejudices and interests.

3. **The 'a priori' method**. This is the method of 'common sense' or 'it stands to reason'. If enough people say something is true, it must be. People in the Middle Ages believed the earth was flat. If it were not, then everyone would have fallen off! Much of psychological knowledge seems to be just 'common sense'. Scientific research may find it to be true, but on the other hand it may not. For instance, we should expect group decisions to be relatively sensible ones, but Stoner (1961) discovered that decisions made by groups tended to be more risky than those made by individuals – a phenomenon known as the **risky shift**. Common sense may be misleading.

So how does scientific method differ from these routes to knowledge? To answer this question it is necessary to look in detail at the characteristics of the scientific approach.

SECTION I SCIENCE AND THE SCIENTIFIC METHOD

What is Science?

Science is the route to knowledge at present favoured by psychologists. There is a set of aims and assumptions in science, shared by scientists in other areas of knowledge. Psychologists must show that they share these aims and assumptions if their use of this route to knowledge is to be justified.

The Aims of Science

The four main interrelated aims of science are **description**, **prediction**, **understanding** and **control**. We now examine each of these in turn.

Description

The most basic scientific aim is to achieve an objective description of events. Scientific description should be as free as possible from bias arising from personal values and interests. Human observers will rarely, if ever, achieve totally unprejudiced description, but that is the goal.

Prediction

Objective description is the foundation for prediction. Where enough information can be gained about an event, and that event follows a pattern, then prediction is possible, which in turn enhances the status and credibility of the knowledge gained. For example, psychologists may observe that those children who frequently watch violent programmes on television are highly aggressive in their own behaviour. The prediction may then be made that the more exposure a child has to violence on television, the more aggressive that child will be. Research may verify or refute this.

Understanding

After accurate prediction the scientist aims to understand cause and effect. It may be that exposure to TV violence directly influences the degree of aggressive behaviour, but why is this so? One suggestion is that aggressive behaviour is acquired through imitation; on the other hand some children may be naturally more aggressive than others and these children prefer violent television. A new set of predictions has to be set up and tested to gain a better understanding of the mechanisms involved.

Control

If we can predict that children exposed to a diet of TV violence will be more aggressive, and we understand this to be the result of imitation, we can control their behaviour by altering the content of what they watch. The control of human behaviour, though, is not that simple. There are also complicated ethical considerations.

The Assumptions of Science

Scientists make common assumptions also about the natural world. There are four key assumptions: **order**, **determinism**, **empiricism** and **parsimony**.

Order

Scientists share the belief that events in the world are not random but ordered. It is therefore possible to find regularities and patterns and so formulate laws. In the case of psychology it is assumed that it is possible to formulate laws of behaviour.

Determinism

If there is order in events then it makes sense to assume that no event ever happens without a reason – it is always determined by something. Psychologists talk about two kinds of determinism – environmental and biological – and endeavour to discover the role that each of these plays in determining thought and behaviour (see Chapter 3, Section II). This implies that no psychological event is irrational. There must be a cause which will eventually be found.

Empiricism

Empiricism derives from a Greek word meaning experience. Scientists believe that it is better to rely on direct sensory experience as a source of evidence than upon introspection, faith or hearsay, which are not open to validation by others. Empirical evidence is open to public scrutiny and can be used to settle disputes about the superiority of one belief over another. Inconsistent observations will eventually be discarded; consistent ones will be retained.

Parsimony

If there are two explanations for an event, and one accounts for all the known facts in a more economical way than the other, then it is favoured as being more parsimonious. A good parsimonious explanation does not go beyond the available empirical evidence and there are as few contradictory elements in it as possible. Behaviourism is often held up as a good example of parsimonious theory; psychoanalysis is not.

Characteristics of Scientific Method

Scientific method is not just concerned with the way data are collected, but is also concerned with the way in which theories are formulated and used. Most importantly methods of data collection need to be objective and theories need to be systematically tested and refined.

In the information which follows, the laboratory experiment features as the clearest example of the scientific approach to data collection. Other methods are described in Chapter 4. They may be equally valid and scientific.

Objectivity

A feature of scientific method is that data are collected in an objective way. There are three ways in which objectivity can be maximised: **control**, **operational definition** and **replication**.

Control   In an experiment one key variable is manipulated (the independent variable or IV); the effects of that manipulation on another variable (the dependent variable or DV) are observed and measured. All other variables are held constant. This is the essence of experimental design.

For example, imagine that you wish to assess the effect of alcohol consumption on driving ability. You could compare scores on a driving test under two conditions: (1) under the influence of alcohol and (2) without alcohol. Alcohol is the IV; driving ability the DV.

It is necessary to control all extraneous variables, to make quite sure that any differences in the DV are due to the IV and not to some other variable (a confounding variable). Because it is not possible to get rid of extraneous variables altogether, the researcher would ensure that they affected both conditions of the experiment equally, balancing each other.

In the example above, extraneous variables to be controlled might include previous driving experience, driving record, driver's previous alcohol consumption, eyesight, age, type of car driven in the test and test difficulty.

It would also seem to be important to make sure that all drivers consumed the same amount of liquid before the test. One group might have alcohol-free lager, the other lager. A further control might be to use a **single** or **double blind** technique – described in Chapter 4 – so that neither the participants, nor the people administering the tests, could influence the results. The participants might not be told whether or not their drink contained alcohol (single blind). In addition, the assistants of the experimenter who assessed the participants' driving ability might not know the hypothesis being tested (double blind).

Operational definition   Scientific method requires precision in defining terms. Concepts such as fatigue, deprivation, attractiveness, anxiety etc used by psychologists need to be carefully defined so that they can be measured. If a psychologist hypothesises that examination performance is affected by anxiety it is necessary to define precisely what is meant by examination performance, what is meant by anxiety and how they will be measured, otherwise replication would be difficult and scientific research would lose its status.

Replicability This means that, if a piece of research is repeated, the findings obtained will be the same or similar. This gives us confidence that the results are reliable. Unless the results are replicable, they will be useless in helping us to build up know-ledge; nor would anyone want to risk using unreliable results in any wider context.

Research is therefore reported in a painstaking way so that replication can be done. This is the only way to check that results obtained are not a one-off or a fluke. Even then scientists do not talk of having proved something, only of having substantial evidence for it.

Methods of replication include using the same participants on different occasions and using different participants in a repeat of the investigation. If similar results are obtained in different contexts they become more convincing and can be used to build up a body of knowledge or a theory.

The Use of Theory

A psychological theory is a general system for explaining the underlying principles of behaviour. The whole process of gather-ing knowledge leads to the construction of theories and this is the second hallmark of the scientific method.

Research and theory stimulate one another through processes of **induction** and **deduction**. Induction involves observing regularities or patterns in empirical data. These are then summarised and integrated into a coherent whole. Deduction involves deriving testable statements from a theory. These are known as **hypotheses**. The process is known as the hypothetico-deductive method and it is cyclical and self-perpetuating. The theory is used as a guiding framework for research so that it can be carried out systematically. The theory is changed and refined all the time in the light of empirical evidence. Figure 6.1 illustrates the hypothetico-deductive method.

The implication of this is that psychology can only employ scientific method if its theories qualify by being testable and therefore refutable, parsimonious and a fertile source of new

FIGURE 6.1
The Hypothetico-Deductive Method of Theory Formation

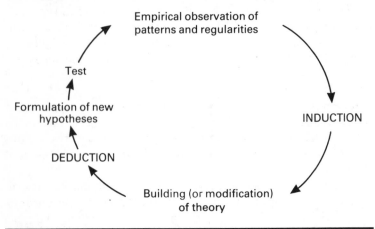

hypotheses. (Refutability, in the eyes of Popper (1972), is a hallmark of a scientific theory. He argues that we should adopt a critical attitude to theories and attempt to refute them, since it is all too easy to interpret data in ways which support theory.) Good scientific theories emerge from the testing process as valid and reliable. This improves their powers of prediction and therefore their practical value. Psychological theories do not always meet these stringent criteria.

Applying the Scientific Method in Psychology

The overwhelming problem for psychologists in using the scientific method lies in their subject matter – human beings. It is not always possible to prevent the participants from exerting their influence on the findings of research, and researchers as well can exert an influence on their findings without knowing they are doing so. These sources of bias have become so well known that they have become a research area in their own right. This is referred to as the 'Social Psychology of the Experiment'. Thus the aims of science are much more difficult to realise, given the special nature of psychological research.

The Social Psychology of the Experiment

There has already been some discussion of these issues in Chapter 4, but it is so important that further discussion is justified. All research is affected to a greater or lesser extent by the situation in which it takes place, the participants involved and the experimenters.

The influence of the situation   Human participants are affected by the fact that they are being observed. They will weigh up the experimental situation for themselves and react accordingly. Orne (1962) used the term **demand characteristics** to mean those cues in the experimental situation to which a participant might respond. These include: (1) the physical set-up of the experiment, (2) the experimenter's behaviour and (3) anything which might alert the participant to the hypothesis being tested.

In an experiment to explore these effects Orne and Evans (1967) found that, out of 18 participants, 15 were prepared to pick up a snake they were told was poisonous, retrieve a coin by plunging a hand into fuming 'nitric acid' and throw the acid into the face of an experimenter. None of these actions would have been likely outside the experimental situation. What is more, participants maintained that they suspected no deception. Tedeschi *et al.* (1985) suggested this might have been due to what they called 'a pact of ignorance'. Participants think they have caught on to the experimenter's hypothesis but do not let the experimenter know, either to save face, or so as not to spoil the experiment. Whatever the reasons, the experimental situation can alter the participants' behaviour in so many ways that the goal of objectivity is not achieved and the participants' behaviour gives no indication of how they would normally behave.

The influence of the participant   Participants can affect the objectivity of research in two ways, according to who they are and what they do.

1. Who are the participants in psychological research? A recurrent criticism of psychology has been that participants in experiments are predominantly white, male, American undergraduates. Tedeschi *et al.* (1985) found that in each year

between 1969 and 1979 a minimum of 70 per cent of social psychology research projects used college students. The balance is being redressed by cross-cultural and sub-cultural research; and this is desirable as science is concerned with general laws and not with findings which can only be applied to a narrow range of people.

Also important is the fact that many of these participants are volunteers (see Chapter 4, Section I). Ora (1965) found that volunteers were more easily influenced, moody, in need of approval, aggressive and neurotic than non-volunteers. Again they are untypical of the population at large, so that generalisations are less easily made.

2. Participants' behaviour in a research situation. Weber and Cook (1972) identified four roles which participants (subjects) might adopt:

   (a) the 'faithful' subject who tries to react to the situation as naturally as possible, whether deliberately or out of disinterest;
   (b) the co-operative subject who tries to discover the hypothesis being tested in order to help prove it;
   (c) the negativistic subject who tries to discover the hypothesis in order to disprove it; and
   (d) the evaluatively apprehensive subject who believes the experimenter is capable of uncovering some hidden truth about them and does as much as possible to avoid being negatively evaluated.

   The faithful subject is clearly the most desirable, but it is not always possible to know which stance is being adopted. Research objectivity may again be threatened and with it the suitability of scientific method for collecting knowledge about humans.

The influence of the experimenter Robert Rosenthal (1969) has conducted a number of classic pieces of research into the influence of the experimenter on research results. He discovered three problems:

1. The biosocial or physical characteristics of the experimenter, such as age, sex, race or appearance, may arouse participants'

prejudices and stereotypes, and may affect the way they respond to different experimenters.

2. There are also psychosocial factors which have to do with the experimenter's social skills in dealing with participants. They may feel at ease with a helpful and friendly experimenter and will co-operate; on the other hand, they may find the experimenter off-putting.

3. Finally there are experimenter expectancy effects. Experimenters who have a hypothesis in mind may end up validating it, simply because of their belief about the way the results will turn out. The hypothesis thus becomes a self-fulfilling prophecy. This again is fully discussed in Chapter 4.

The Standing of Psychological Theories

As stated earlier, part of the scientific method has to do with the way in which theories are used. In psychology, unusually among sciences, the same phenomenon can be explained from a number of theoretical viewpoints. (Different approaches are more fully discussed in Chapter 2 of this book.) The scientific method should eventually weed out those theories which are less open to testing. The relationship of different approaches to the scientific method is briefly discussed below.

Introspection

In the early days of psychology data were gathered in the form of introspections made in carefully controlled conditions, an approach advocated by Wundt (1879) (see Chapter 1, Section II). It proved very difficult to achieve the aims of operational definition and replicability, in spite of attempts to control such things as stimuli and instructions to participants. Introspection also failed because the data were not empirical.

Psychoanalysis

The psychoanalytical approach of Sigmund Freud had similar problems in adopting the scientific method. The subject matter, the workings of the unconscious mind, is not publicly observable or easily defined. There is also difficulty with control and replicability. The assumptions of order and determinism are met, but those of parsimony and empiricism less easily. Attempts have been made to test psychoanalysis experimentally, but opponents argue that the theory is not suitable for scientific testing as it is often irrefutable – the theory can account for apparently contradictory research evidence.

Behaviourism

The behaviourist school (Watson, 1919) has possibly been most successful in applying scientific method in psychology. Behaviourists rejected earlier approaches and advocated instead publicly observable behaviour as the proper subject matter for psychology. Their research was, and still is, characterised by rigorous control, operational definition and replicability. The four assumptions of science – order, determinism, empiricism and parsimony – are accepted as central. Behaviourist theories are a source of readily testable hypotheses because the subject matter lends itself to testing. For all its shortcomings, as a source of scientifically researched data, the behaviourist approach has few equals in psychology.

Humanistic Psychology

Because the humanistic approach takes conscious experience as the focus of its attention it encounters problems similar to those of introspection and psychoanalysis. Scientific testing is not easy, at least in part because it lacks a coherent theory to work from. Carl Rogers, the founder of the humanistic school, made great strides towards more systematic testing of humanistic ideas towards the end of his career. In particular, he developed Q-sort techniques (devised by Stephenson in 1953) as a way of assessing the effectiveness of the client-centred therapy which he advocated – work which has been continued by his successors. However one of the central tenets of the approach is that scientific method is not the best route to knowledge about humans: the only meaningful way to understand them is to see the world from each person's unique perspective. Since a person's inner world is not open to public scrutiny, observations could never be empirical.

Humanistic psychologists reject determinism in favour of free will (see also Chapter 3), preferring to see humans exercising choice over their actions. Thus assumptions of order and parsimony are untenable. Finally they reject experimentation as a means of finding out about humans. The method itself is seen as dehumanising and reductionist, and the use of the term 'subjects' as reflecting a lack of recognition of the human being. (There is a discussion of reductionism in Chapter 3.)

Conclusion

To summarise the above arguments, if a discipline aims to describe, understand, predict and control, and if the assumptions of order, determinism, empiricism and parsimony can be met, then scientific method is suitable.

Psychology does not either wholly fail or wholly succeed in meeting these criteria. The question of suitability is inextricably linked with the way one defines science. If it is defined by its aims then, on the whole, psychology is scientific. If it is defined by its assumptions then some approaches to psychology fit the mould more comfortably than others.

Even if it is assumed that the aims and assumptions of science are appropriate in psychology, the special nature of the subject matter and the researcher's relationship to it creates difficulties in conducting research objectively. However psychologists are not alone in having problems in achieving objectivity. All scientists are human beings, whose personal values and biases will be reflected in the way in which they select and interpret information. If we dismissed psychology as being inappropriate for scientific method because of objectivity problems, then other scientific disciplines would also have to suffer the same fate.

Turning to the way in which theories are built and tested, it can be said that, while psychologists do achieve this by using scientific method, different schools of psychology focus upon different types of subject matter, some of which are more easily operationally defined and tested than others. While behaviourists find scientific method very suitable for their purpose, humanistic psychologists reject that most scientific of methods, the experiment.

The philosopher Thomas Kuhn (1962) claims that psychology lacks a uniting *paradigm*, an essential characteristic of a mature science. (A paradigm is a set of assumptions about what should be studied and how. It is a common or global perspective, such as Darwinism in biology). According to Valentine (1982) behaviourism is the closest psychology has come to having a paradigm. In fact Kuhn asserts that until psychology has a paradigm it is not science but pre-science. If this is accepted then to ask questions about the suitability of the scientific method in psychology is premature. Some psychologists do seem to be able to apply scientific method more easily than others. This does not mean that knowledge collected in other ways has no value; it is just that the scientific method in psychology is particularly favoured, regardless of arguments against its suitability. It is interesting to note that, when Sigmund Freud was a young man in the latter part of the nineteenth century, the scientific route to knowledge was relatively new and caused great excitement. It is just conceivable that in the future the scientific method may not enjoy the status it has today.

Self-assessment Questions

1. What routes to knowledge are there apart from the scientific method?
2. What are the aims and assumptions of the scientific method?
3. What are the characteristics of the scientific method?
4. Can the scientific method be applied in psychology?

SECTION II PSYCHOLOGICAL RESEARCH AND THE USE OF ANIMALS

Next to the ethical considerations surrounding human participants in psychological research there can be few issues more emotive than the use of animals in experimentation. Recently this area has attracted renewed attention from the media because the existing legislation governing the use of animals in this way (drawn up in 1876) has undergone a long-overdue revision. Research is now governed by the Animals (Scientific Procedures) Act 1986, which protects living vertebrates.

Psychological research is only one of the many ways in which animals are used by humans, but it has received its fair share of adverse publicity. The student is encouraged to examine some of the readily available anti-vivisectionist and animal liberation literature and to consider its claims in the light of what is presented here.

The following questions will be addressed: (1) how do psychologists justify their use of animals; (2) what practical use is animal research to psychologists and (3) what are the practical and ethical issues in animal experimentation?

How Do Psychologists Justify Their Use of Animals?

Broadbent (1961) justifies the use of animals in psychological research in three main ways:

1. If it is assumed, as in Darwin's view, that all species are biologically related to each other through evolution, then it can be argued that their behaviour patterns are also related. The notion of 'continuity' between species is also discussed in Chapter 1. Just as human autonomy can be understood by reference to other species, so can human behaviour. Humans differ from other animals in complexity only, so much can be learned about them by making comparisons with simpler species.
2. Many laboratory experiments which are carried out on animals would not be permitted with humans for ethical reasons. Examples are controlled interbreeding experiments (for research into genetic correlates of behaviour), various kinds of deprivation (social, maternal, perceptual, sensory) and brain and tissue research.
3. One of the standard techniques of science is to study simpler systems in order to understand more complex ones. If we accept the notion of continuity between animal species (as in (1) above) then studies of the behaviour and nervous systems of animals could reveal a great deal about humans.

To these three points, two more can be added:

4. Animals make convenient participants for several reasons. They reproduce rapidly, so the effects of early experience and

selective breeding can quickly be assessed. Heredity and environment can be precisely controlled in nature–nurture research. Emotional involvement with animal participants is also less likely than with humans, so the experimenter's objectivity is improved.
5. Animal experiments can be useful in the early stages of research as a means of generating hypotheses for subsequent testing on humans. Alternatively research findings which are only suggestive or correlational in nature with humans could be tested experimentally on animals in order to isolate cause and effect.

Practical Applications of Animal Research in Psychology

In 1985, Neal Miller published a detailed article describing research on animals which he considers to be valuable. This was, at least in part, a response to various animal rights groups who, he said, could mislead people with 'grossly false statements' about animal research. Rather than helping animals, he says, their actions impede research which is beneficial to both animals and humans. He suggests that such groups' energies could be more usefully directed towards fighting for the conservation of endangered species or towards raising funds for refuges for abandoned or mistreated animals.

Miller notes the ways in which animal research has benefited animals. For example, a better understanding of the behaviour of animals which damage crops or carry disease has led to the development of deterrents (such as specially designed 'scarecrows', Conover, 1982), thus doing away with the need for lethal control. Animal research has also helped in the preservation of endangered species and has done much to promote the health of domestic pets. From a psychological point of view, research into animal learning stands out as being of great practical use to humans. Some examples will serve to illustrate this contribution.

Treatment of Nocturnal Enuresis

In 1938, Mowrer and Mowrer used principles derived from Pavlov's experiments on classical conditioning in dogs to develop an alarm blanket for the treatment of persistent night-time bed-wetting in children. As soon as moisture touches the blanket, an alarm sounds and wakes the child just as he has started to urinate. The bell is normally associated with waking but the sensation of a full bladder is not. Conditioning helps the child to learn the new behaviour of waking when the bladder is full with repeated presentations of the bell at the appropriate time. Soon the sensation of a full bladder becomes associated with the response of waking up, the bell will no longer be necessary and the child is able to avoid wetting the bed. Apart from the obvious benefits to be had from the disappearance of the enuresis, Mowrer and Mowrer found that children treated successfully improve in other ways too. For example, teachers noted improvements in various aspects of such children's personality and behaviour even though the teachers were not aware that the children had been enuretic.

Life Saving

Pigeons have been trained to detect coloured life rafts against the background of the sea through the use of operant conditioning techniques derived from Skinner's work (Simmons, 1981). Pigeons can be trained to peck discs of different colours to earn food rewards and they will generalise this training to new situations. In tests their keen vision enabled them to detect 85 per cent of life raft targets, compared to the 50 per cent detected by helicopter crews.

Teaching Machines and Programmed Learning

Derived from operant conditioning principles, educational materials of various kinds can be programmed into computers to aid learning. In addition experiments with chimps using computers to communicate have helped to develop communication systems for autistic and retarded children.

Behaviour Change

Walker (1984) draws a distinction between *behaviour therapy* (based on classical conditioning) and *behaviour modification* (based on operant conditioning). Both are derived from experiments using animals and have been used to explain and treat some kinds of mental disorder. The classic case of Little Albert (Watson and Rayner, 1920), who was conditioned to fear a white rat, spawned a variety of behaviour therapy techniques for the treatment of phobias including systematic desensitisation, flooding and implosion. Another technique derived from classical conditioning is aversion therapy. Lang and Melamed (1969) described how this had been used to save the life of a nine-month-old baby who was malnourished and dehydrated through persistent, ruminative vomiting (regurgitation and rechewing of food). After all other treatments had failed, the therapists trained the infant to develop a conditioned aversion to vomiting by applying a series of one second-long electric shocks to his calf whenever he showed signs of regurgitation. The infant learned not to vomit in order to avoid the shock, and subsequently he made a complete recovery.

Behaviour modification also has many applications in clinical settings. In one case described by Isaacs, Thomas and Goldiamond (1960) a schizophrenic man, who had been mute for years, was gradually trained to speak again by using behaviour shaping procedures, with chewing gum as a reinforcer.

Animal Helpers

Pfaffenberger (1963) was able to improve on the efficiency of guide dogs for the blind through selective breeding and by applying research findings concerned with the most sensitive periods for learning in a puppy's life. Capuchin monkeys have been trained to be home helps for disabled and paralysed people. Monkeys can learn to serve drinks with a straw, place a magazine on a reading stand, open and close doors, operate lifts and carry out a variety of other tasks for the reward of food or fruit juice dispensed by the disabled person.

In view of these examples and many other areas of research using animals, Miller concludes that there is a strong case for continuing to back it – both financially and morally.

Practical and Ethical Aspects of Animal Experimentation

So far the case for animal experimentation has been strongly stated. Here some of the practical and ethical objections which have been raised will be considered, along with the replies which psychologists have given.

Practical Considerations

Practical considerations have two main themes. The first concerns whether it is reasonable to transfer (extrapolate) findings from animals to humans and the second concerns more general objections about the experimental method itself. Anti-extrapolationists emerge from a number of camps:

1. **Humanistic psychologists** would argue that the human condition is unique; that is, that humans are qualitatively different as well as quantitatively different from animals.
2. Those who disagree with Darwin's theory of evolution, on religious grounds for instance, would make the same assertion.
3. Koestler (1970) argued that to transfer findings from rats to humans was to commit the sin of **ratomorphism**.
4. Others argue that there is a danger that researchers may be unable to adopt an objective view of their animal participants, so that they attribute them with human qualities for which there is no real evidence; this is known as **anthropomorphism**.
5. Animal rights campaigners may well draw on cases where extrapolation of findings about drugs from one species to another has been inappropriate. The implication of this is that, if physiological reactions to the same chemical differ so much between species, how can we be confident in transferring findings about behaviour from one to another?

Regarding the experimental method, objections centre on the degree of control exerted in the laboratory experiment. There is no doubt that the precision achieved is one of the strengths of the method, but it is also its greatest weakness. Laboratory experiments are said to lack **ecological validity**; that is, they do not relate to the real world. There are some forms of experimentation, such as the field or natural type, which are not affected by the problems of a controlled environment but, although realism is gained, control is lost.

Ethical Considerations

In 1986, the Experimental Psychology Society issued some guidelines to assist in the planning of experiments on animals.

1. In general, they say researchers have an 'obligation to avoid, or

at least minimise, discomfort to all living animals.'
2. Psychologists are also obliged to know the law in relation to animal research and to acquire the necessary Home Office certification before proceeding. (Applications for licences to conduct animal research are not met lightly, so proposed projects must be of the highest quality as well as justifiable on practical grounds. Licences are only given to suitably qualified people.)
3. The guidelines also advise psychologists to be thoroughly familiar with the needs of the species being studied, and to be as economical as possible in the numbers used.

A number of psychologists have published articles in defence of animal experimentation, not only because of the recent review of the relevant legislation, but also because attacks by animal liberationists and anti-vivisectionists have stung them into reply.

In the article by Miller (1985) reviewed earlier, some statistics are presented which illustrate the relatively low occurrence of animal research. Coile and Miller (1984) reviewed articles published in American Psychological Association journals in the previous five years. Of the 608 articles examined, only 7 per cent of the contents reported research primarily on animals, while 93 per cent concerned humans. No instances of the kind of research claimed to be commonplace by animal rights groups were found. Miller quotes evidence to show that far more abuse of pets and farm animals occurs than in any research facility and claims that the energies of animal rights campaigners could be usefully directed elsewhere. In 1987, Jeffrey Gray added his opinions to the debate in a paper entitled 'The ethics and politics of animal experimentation'. He was writing in response to attacks by the British Union for the Abolition of Vivisection (BUAV), and these are some of the points he made:

1. He claims that BUAV selects psychological research as a soft target because it lacks the powerful backing of the medical establishment. BUAV quotes selectively from scientific papers in such a way that research looks pointless. In reality such research, as we have seen, can be significant in treating and preventing a variety of disorders in humans.

2. Because the aims, methods and findings from animal psychology research are not always easily understood by the lay person, distorted liberationist literature is more easily grasped by comparison and is therefore more believable.
3. Given the widespread use of animals by humans, says Gray, why single out experimentation as particularly vicious or unworthy? To take BUAV's argument to its logical limits would be to ban all use of animals by humans. Therefore liberationists need to moderate their position. The standard adopted by most people and scientists is to minimise animals' suffering and to weigh up the costs to them against the benefit to mankind. To ban any activity involving animal suffering would be both unrealistic and politically unpopular.
4. Gray is particularly critical of the way anti-vivisectionists publicise their point of view, using emotive images which are not representative of the bulk of animal research. In addition careful choice of words in their literature can give the impression that experimenters gratuitously inflict suffering on their experimental participants and enjoy themselves in the process!
5. As a final comment, Gray draws attention to the fact that a structure of committees decides whether public funds should be used for research and, since competition for funding is fierce, projects must be extremely well designed, potentially very useful, and in line with Home Office rulings. The general public are not always aware of these safeguards, or of the objectivity of committee members, and would probably be much more reassured if they were.

In an attempt to resolve the problem of animal experimentation, Bateson (1986), who accepts the importance of such research, says that a definition of suffering needs to be made by both sides. He suggests, as a starting-point, three important issues which a committee made up of research scientists, animal welfare representatives and disinterested parties should consider in deciding whether a research proposal should be accepted: (1) certainty of medical benefit, (2) the quality of the research, and (3) the degree of animal suffering involved. If the first two were high and the third low then the research would probably be permitted. The committee's most important function would be in deciding how to proceed in different circumstances, as when animal suffering was likely to be high but the quality of research and the certainty of medical benefit were also high.

Alternatives to Animal Experimentation

If the arguments against animal experimentation are accepted, we are left with the problem of finding acceptable ways of studying animal behaviour which give research findings of comparable quality to rigorously controlled laboratory techniques. So what can be done?

A possible alternative is to use ethological methods and study animals, as far as possible, in their natural habitat. One problem with the ethological approach is that it tends to see instinctive (unlearned) behaviour as central; therefore it would be unsuitable for highly controlled laboratory experiments of the kind which look at learned behaviour. In addition, any research which was reductionist in nature would not lend itself readily to ethological methods. Experimentation obviously has a place, and can work well as a complement to ethological approaches, since both have strengths and weaknesses.

Secondly, there are detailed accounts of alternatives to animal experimentation in medical research (such as tissue research and in vitro techniques) but much of the content does not apply to psychological research.

Thirdly, there is some scope for computer simulations of behaviour, particularly in the field of cognition but, again, these do not suit all areas of enquiry.

As a final note, it is worth considering the rationale which ultimately underlies all animal research: that some forms of life are more valuable than others. In the field of human research, some unscrupulous scientists used Second World War prisoners in their investigations of germ warfare and the limits of human endurance. This was not because the scientists were opposed to animal research but because they sensed a rare opportunity to utilise humans at will. There is much debate about the ethics of using the findings from such research because of the suffering involved. Perhaps the same reasoning should be applied to the use of animal research findings.

Self-assessment Questions

1. On what grounds do psychologists justify the use of animals in research?
2. How has animal research benefited humans?
3. What are the practical and ethical objections to animal research?
4. What alternatives to animal research are there?

SECTION III ETHICS IN PSYCHOLOGICAL RESEARCH AND PRACTICE

Fortunately for psychologists, much of their research and practice does not raise ethical problems since it is possible to inform people fully of the procedures involved. Problems only arise when it is felt to be necessary to withhold information or to subject people to risk.

Until the 1960s there was little in the way of ethical guidelines for psychologists. Now there are codes of conduct and ethical principles for use in many different contexts. For example, the British Psychological Society has compiled a list of ethical principles for research with human participants (1990) and a code of conduct for psychologists (1985). These are intended to ensure that the highest ethical standards are maintained in both research and practice.

The various guidelines unite psychologists in reminding them that their aims should be to 'ameliorate the human condition and enhance human dignity' (BPS, 1978). However, as with any ethical code, the emphasis is on the word 'guidelines' – they are open to interpretation.

In this section some of the central ethical issues in research will be considered, examples being taken from the field of social psychology. In the area of practice, techniques of behaviour change will be the focus of attention.

Ethics and Research with Humans

Ethical Guidelines

The main points of the BPS's own guidelines for research with human participants can be summarised as follows:

1. If psychologists are to continue to enjoy the freedom they currently have in their research, and the goodwill of potential participants, then they should respond by ensuring that their research is competent, non-wasteful, objective and ethical.
2. Psychologists must make their research results available to the public and colleagues but, at the same time, ensure that they are not misunderstood or misused. If it is felt to be necessary to restrict access to findings, there must be good reason for this (such as national security) and the opinions of disinterested and experienced colleagues should be sought before deciding on this course of action.
3. The psychological community is answerable to itself, the law and the public and has an obligation to monitor its own standards of conduct. This means that psychologists should consider both the scientific worth of their research and its possible impact on the participants who take part and the attitudes of the general public.

Further guidance is given on specific issues. This covers informing the participants, the use of deception, the status of volunteers, confidentiality, safety and the use of children. Professional responsibility is emphasised throughout. These issues can be more conveniently arranged under two headings, 'Risks' and 'Informed Consent'.

Risks

1. The most obvious form of risk a participant is likely to encounter is some form of **psychological stress**, such as fear, anxiety, embarrassment, guilt or loss of self-esteem. Psychologists have an ethical obligation to avoid causing these, as far as is possible, and to protect participants from unforeseen risk. This may mean abandoning or redesigning the research.
2. A less obvious form of risk arises from **coercion** of participants to take part in research. This is especially important when they are not self-selected volunteers and are offered payment or other perks for their co-operation. Participants may feel obliged to take part in the research because of these.

3. **Deception** is another form of risk. It may be necessary to withhold information from participants for a variety of reasons; for example, it could make a nonsense of the experiment if they knew the hypothesis being tested. If there is no alternative to deception, and the research is important enough to warrant it, then the researcher should debrief the participants afterwards in order to ensure that there has been no lasting harm.

4. Finally, if **breaches of confidentiality** or privacy have occurred, measures must be taken to ensure the anonymity of participants and, if it is possible, to give them the option to withhold their data. Sometimes the latter would not be possible. For example, Humphreys (1970) was able to conduct research into homosexual acts in public toilets by acting as a look-out for the participants. While the breach of privacy is obvious, it could be argued that the participants had, in a sense, granted the researcher permission to observe them.

Informed Consent

Informed consent is a second key issue in research because it is not always desirable to inform participants fully; nor is the researcher always in a position to do so, for instance if the research is into new areas. Even with the best of intentions, the researcher may fail to inform participants fully because they are told too little or they fail to understand.

If the researcher feels that it is necessary to proceed without obtaining informed consent there are two further possibilities: a pilot study could be used and participants could be interviewed afterwards about how acceptable they found the procedure; alternatively role-playing could be used, where fully informed participants act out the procedures. The latter was used by Zimbardo (1973) in a now famous prison simulation exercise.

Examples of Ethically Questionable Research

The reader will probably be familiar with some examples of social psychology research which have been attacked on ethical grounds and which have been defended on the basis of their contribution to knowledge. For example, Solomon Asch's (1956) classic conformity experiments are well known, and there are a number of 'bystander apathy' experiments. These all involved some deception of the participants and, in some cases, considerable stress, but could be justified on the basis of what was learned about group influence. Accounts of such research can be found in most introductory social psychology texts.

In the context of ethical issues, the most frequently quoted are Stanley Milgram's 'obedience to authority' research (1974) and Philip Zimbardo *et al.*'s (1973) prison simulation. Detailed accounts of these are easily found (for example, see Gross, 1987) so only the briefest details are necessary here. Milgram's research centred on the extent to which people would obey authority. Volunteer participants were recruited and tested individually. A cover story was necessary to lead them to believe that, during the experiment, it was necessary to give increasingly painful electric shocks to another person who was out of sight in the next room. As the voltage of the shocks increased, the other person made sounds indicating increasing distress until eventually there was an ominous silence. The other person was a stooge and the shocks were not real.

The fact that 65 per cent of the participants were prepared to continue to shock to the end of the voltage scale surprised Milgram, especially as the learner had made no response after a certain shock level. However, many of the participants were clearly upset by the experiment and showed reactions ranging from nervous laughter to full-blown uncontrollable seizures.

After the experiment was over, Milgram went to great lengths to debrief the participants. He reunited them with the 'learner' to convince them that no harm had been done. He held post-experimental interviews and reassured participants that their reactions were not unusual and he followed them up afterwards to check that no long-term damage had been done. In spite of all these precautions, Milgram's work has come under attack, as we shall see.

Zimbardo's intention was to conduct a two week-long study of social and situational factors affecting reactions to prison life. Young male volunteers were randomly assigned to play the role of prisoner or guard in a mock-up prison in the basement of one of Stanford University's buildings. None of the participants had any training for these roles. Each received $15 a day for taking part. Events in the prison were monitored continuously. In a very short time the prisoners attempted a rebellion, but this was crushed by the guards. After this the prisoners became increasingly passive and the guards more aggressive. In less than 36 hours one of the prisoners was released because of uncontrollable crying, fits of rage, disorganised thinking and severe depression. Others had to be released over the next few days because of a variety of stress symptoms.

Zimbardo stopped the project after only six days because of its effects on the prisoners. Like Milgram, he subsequently found himself defending his case against complaints that his research was unethical.

Weighing up Costs and Benefits

When questions are raised about ethical aspects of research, it is usually necessary to weigh the costs (such as risks to the participants, the researcher and the reputation of psychology) against the benefits (for example, important theoretical or practical advances).

Can Milgram's research be defended in terms of costs and benefits? Certainly his findings appear to be significant, but what of the ethical question? Concerning this, **Baumrind (1964)** has been a vociferous critic. Baumrind's criticisms centre mainly on whether enough was done to protect the participants from harm. Milgram had found it necessary to deceive them and to put them through procedures which many found stressful; that is, causing pain to another person. He prodded them to go on when they expressed a wish to withdraw. In reply, Milgram puts forward the following arguments:

1. He could not have known in advance how far participants would be prepared to obey his instructions or the degree of discomfort this would cause them. He felt they were given ample opportunity to withdraw if they wanted to.
2. Before the experiment, he had 'piloted' the procedure by asking 14 psychology students and 40 professors to estimate what a sample of 100 participants would do. They estimated that most participants would stop about halfway through and only one or two would go right to the end. Admittedly Milgram did not ask people like those he eventually used but he had tried to anticipate problems.

3. Milgram defends his case on the basis of the debriefing procedures he followed afterwards. The participants were reassured that they had not delivered electric shocks to the 'learner' and they had a long discussion about what had happened with the 'learner' and the experimenter. All participants were reassured that the feelings they had experienced were similar to those of other participants. Later they were all given a detailed account of the procedures and the results.

Of particular interest are the responses to a post-experiment questionnaire which participants filled in. This gave them a chance to express their feelings about having taken part. Some 84 per cent said that they were 'very glad' or 'glad' to have taken part; 15 per cent were 'neutral' and only 1.3 per cent said they were 'sorry' or 'very sorry' to have taken part. Of the participants 80 per cent thought that there should be more research of this kind and 74 per cent claimed to have learned something of personal value. In fact, a year after the experiment, Milgram received a letter from one of the participants who said that he had learned how important it was not to harm another person even if this meant disobeying authority.

In the end Milgram seems to have satisfied himself that the means of his research justified the ends, and he was careful to follow ethical guidelines when events took an unexpected turn. What is more, the majority of the participants seem to have benefited from the experience in the longer term.

Zimbardo also found himself defending his case after publication of his study. He responded with an assessment of the costs and benefits involved in the research (1973):

1. He acknowledges freely that participants role-playing 'prisoners', even though they were carefully selected for their stability, suffered 'psychological humiliation, anxiety, perhaps a loss of innocence and extremely unpleasant memories'.
2. On the benefit side there was an advance in social–psychological knowledge, which raised people's consciousness about prison conditions. There were a number of publications and a great deal of publicity (which, subsequently, put enormous strain on Zimbardo's time and personal resources).
3. Like Milgram, Zimbardo dealt carefully with the participants

after the study, using intensive individual interviews, encounter group sessions and follow-up surveys. He was satisfied that the suffering experienced by 'prisoners' was restricted to the somewhat artificial situation. He also claims that many of the participants felt that the experience had been a valuable source of personal insight.

4. Zimbardo also felt that some participants benefited from dealing with the moral dilemmas posed by the research findings. (In Kohlberg's view (1975) this is the best way to raise an individual's level of moral reasoning.) Subsequently some volunteered to work in local prisons and most became interested in prison reform. They also gained financially, and were able to use the experiences in their college courses. Some also enjoyed the notoriety of appearing in *Life* magazine!

Zimbardo feels that his findings are not artefacts of an unusual research setting but, instead, reveal important forces at work in institutions. Far from being worried by criticism, he asserts that responsible psychologists welcome and expect evaluation of their work and methods as a necessary and desirable part of what they do.

Ethics and the Application of Psychological Knowledge

This section concerns means by which psychologists can alter behaviour, acting on what they have learned from research. The emphasis here will be on a selection of behaviourist techniques for behaviour change in clinical settings.

Some critics accuse behaviour modifiers of being manipulative, coercive and controlling, conditioning people against their will into behaviour patterns which they would not necessarily choose. How far is this image of the behaviourist psychologist justified? (See Chapter 2, Section III.)

Behaviour therapy, based on Pavlovian conditioning, includes relatively uncontentious techniques such as systematic desensitisation for phobias and the use of electric alarm blankets for the treatment of persistent nocturnal enuresis. Ethical questions are more likely to be raised where pain or sickness is involved, as in **aversion therapy**.

A well-known example of the power of aversion therapy is

provided by Lang and Melamed (1969). (This study was described above, in connection with applications of animal research.) In this case there is little doubt that aversion therapy saved the child's life. It is the use of pain which is in question.

There are many types of behaviour modification which are based on operant conditioning procedures. Put simply, the idea is that behaviour can be shaped and changed by the controlled use of reinforcement and punishment. One of the best known applications of behaviour modification is the **Token Economy**. In 1968, Ayllon and Azrin introduced into a ward of schizophrenics an economic system whereby tokens could be earned for desirable behaviours such as general hygiene, self-care and work on the ward. Tokens could be saved and exchanged for such things as TV viewing time, cigarettes and sweets, clothes or cosmetics. The principle behind this was that desirable behaviours would increase because they were rewarded. While the system was no cure for schizophrenia, social and self-care skills in long-stay patients did improve considerably. Not only does the behaviour of participants change, but often the morale and enthusiasm of staff improves when they begin to see the beneficial effects of their efforts in implementing a programme.

What is ethically problematic about techniques which are so obviously beneficial? Objections centre on three areas:

1. *The use of punishment and pain.* It has been argued that **punishment** only has a temporary suppressive effect and, as it produces negative reactions in the learner, it is important to have controls against its use. To guard against the free use of electric shock, Miron (1968) suggests psychologists should first try the shock on themselves! This is a form of 'countercontrol' (Skinner, 1971). (However punishment is part of everyday life and treating problem behaviour without it would not teach the patient much about how to cope in the real world.)
2. *Deprivation.* In some behaviour modification procedures it is necessary to **deprive** the experimental participant of reinforcers in order to encourage them to respond. Reinforcement becomes dependent on the appearance of certain behaviours, as in token economies. Token economies fell foul of the critics when some of them appeared to infringe basic human rights, for example when attendance at church, and provision of food

or privacy were made contingent upon the performance of desirable behaviours. While such extreme measures may not be used today, the behaviourists argue that the level of reinforcement on a programme may be higher than that normally experienced by a patient and that not to use such techniques may deprive that person of the chance of rehabilitation.

3. *Free will.* On the subject of free will, criticisms that an approach removes people's freedom to act is a problem for all deterministic approaches. Radical behaviourists would answer that it is not a question of imposing restrictions where none existed before. Their theoretical position is that all behaviour is controlled, so the ethical problem is not whether behaviour should be controlled but who should presume to take control of another and for what ends. In their eyes, behavioural techniques simply make systematic use of the processes already at work in everyday life and people's alarm at their methods results from their recognition of how powerful this can be. (See Chapter 3 for a fuller discussion of free will and determinism.)

There are trends in therapeutic techniques towards turning more control of the situation over to the patient in order to reduce the imbalance of power between him/her and the therapist. For example, in systematic desensitisation the patient would construct their own hierarchy of feared situations with the therapist's help and then have considerable control in the pacing of exposure to them. There are also strict codes of conduct for therapists. All these things help towards 'countercontrol'.

If the wider ethical implications of these treatments are considered, then, in terms of costs and benefits, behaviourism fares well. In certain areas of disorder such as sexual dysfunction, enuresis, nervous tics and habit disorders, treatment is very effective. It can alleviate suffering, improve the quality of life and even save lives.

On a different note, behaviourist treatments are often attacked as ethically unsound because they are said not to treat the root cause of a problem. Radical behaviourists can answer this in two ways:

1. If it is accepted that the problem is the product of faulty learning, then new learning does eradicate the problem.

2. If behaviour is determined by experiences in the environment, then problem behaviour is the result of a faulty environment. It is society, not the individual, which needs to change. This is ultimately a political issue, raising new ethical questions beyond the scope of this chapter.

Conclusion

There are many areas of psychology, not discussed here, where still more ethical concerns are important. The problems involved in various kinds of psychiatric intervention, such as electrical stimulation of the brain, the use of psychoactive drugs and psychosurgery, are relevant to psychology because they are used to treat psychological conditions. Ethical problems are present in any kind of therapy and in any area where psychological knowledge is applied, for example in education, in the workplace and in legal psychology. The field of psychometric testing is particularly relevant in all of these and raises special problems of confidentiality and ownership of information gathered.

In all these a solution to ethical problems would be to adopt one of two extreme positions: either ban all ethically suspect activities altogether, or allow psychologists a completely free hand. Neither of these solutions is practical or rational; consequently psychologists find themselves constantly dealing with ethical dilemmas and defending their position.

Psychological knowledge could not advance without a certain amount of risk, both to the researchers and to the participants, or to psychologists and their clients. If, in the end, as Hawks (1981) asserts, psychologists are working towards the ultimate goal of prevention of psychological problems, rather than cure, ethical risks are a small price to pay along the way.

Self-assessment Questions

1. Summarise the main points of the BPS ethical guidelines.
2. Assess the ethical standing of two pieces of psychological research.
3. Discuss some of the ethical issues involved in applying psychological knowledge.

FURTHER READING

P. Bateson, 'When to Experiment on Animals', *New Scientist*, 109 (1986) 1496, pp. 30–32.

British Psychological Society, *Ethical Principles for Conducting Research with Human Participants* (Leicester: The British Psychological Society, 1990).

S. Fairbairn and G. Fairbairn (eds), *Psychology, Ethics and Change* (London: Routledge & Kegan Paul, 1987).

T.S. Kuhn, *The Structure of Scientific Revolutions* (Chicago: University of Chicago Press, 1962).

N.E. Miller, 'The Value of Behavioral Research on Animals', *American Psychologist*, 40 (1985) pp. 423–40.

A. Wadeley, *Ethics in Psychological Research and Practice* (Leicester: The British Psychological Society, 1991).

G. Westland, *Current Crises in Psychology* (London: Heineman, 1978).

Bibliography

Ainsworth, M.D.S. and S.M. Bell (1969) 'Some contemporary patterns of mother–infant interaction in the feeding situation', in A. Ambrose (ed.), *Stimulation in Early Infancy* (London: Academic Press).

Alexander, B.K., R.B. Coambs and P.F. Hadaway (1978) 'The effect of housing and gender on morphine self-administration in rats'. *Psychopharmacology*, 58, pp. 175–9.

Allport, G.W. (1961) *Pattern and Growth in Personality* (New York: Holt, Reinhart & Winston).

Allport, G.W. (1962) 'The general and unique in psychological science', *Journal of Personality*, 30, pp. 405–21.

Allport, G.W. (1965) *Letters from Jenny* (New York: Harcourt, Brace and World).

Anastasi, A. (1958) in R.M. Lerner (1986) *Concepts and Theories in Human Development*, 2nd edn (New York: Random House).

Animals (Scientific Procedures Act) 1986, *Halsbury's Statutes (4th edn) Current Statutes Service, Issue 9, Vol. 2*, pp. 3–34 (London: Butterworth).

Argyle, M. (1987) *The Psychology of Happiness* (London: Methuen).

Asch, S.E. (1952) *Social Psychology* (New York: Prentice-Hall).

Asch, S.E. (1956) 'Studies of independence and submission to group pressure: a minority of one against a unanimous majority', in *Psychological Monographs*, 70(a).

Atkinson, J.W. (1964) *An Introduction to Motivation* (Princeton, New Jersey: Van Nostrand Reingold).

Atkinson, R.L., R.C. Atkinson, E.E. Smith and E.R. Hilgard (1985) *Introduction to Psychology*, 9th edn (New York: Harcourt Brace Jovanovich).

Atkinson, R.C. and R.M. Shiffrin (1971) 'The control of short-term memory', in *Scientific American*, 224, pp. 82–90.

Ayllon, T. and N.H. Azrin (1968) *The Token Economy: A Motivational System for Therapy and Rehabilitation* (New York: Appleton Century Crofts).

Bach y Rita, P., C.C. Collins, F.A. Saunders, B. White and L. Scadden (1969) 'Visual substitution by tactile image projection', *Nature*, 221, pp. 963–4.

Ball, B. (1989) *Manage your own career* (Leicester: BPS Books).

Bard, P. (1934) 'The neurohumoral basis of emotional reactions', in Murchison, C.A. (ed.) *Handbook of General Experimental Psychology* (Worcester, Mass.: Clark University Press).

Baron-Cohen, S. (1988) 'Social and pragmatic deficits in autism: cognitive or affective?', *Journal of Autism and Developmental Disorders*, vol. 18, pp. 379–402.

Baron-Cohen, S., A.M. Leslie and U. Frith (1985) 'Does the autistic child have a "theory of mind"?' *Cognition*, vol. 21, pp. 37–46.

Bateson, P. (1986) 'When to experiment on animals', *New Scientist*, 109, (1496) pp. 30–2.

Baumrind, D. (1964) 'Some thoughts on the ethics of research after reading Milgram's "Behavioural study of obedience"', *American Psychologist*, 19, pp. 4211–23.

Bell, A.W., J. Costello and D.E. Kuchemann (1983) *A Review of Research in Mathematical Education: research on learning and teaching* (London: NFER).

Bergin, A.E. (1971) 'The evaluation of therapeutic outcomes', in A.E. Bergin and S.L. Garfield (eds), *Handbook of Psychotherapy and Behaviour Change: an Empirical Analysis* (New York: Wiley).

Berlyne, D.E. (1960) *Conflict, Arousal and Curiosity* (New York: McGraw-Hill).

Birch, A. and T. Malim (1988) *Developmental Psychology: from infancy to adulthood* (London: Macmillan).

Blackler, F. and C. Brown (1980) 'Job redesign and social change: case studies at Volvo', in K.D. Duncan, M. Grumeberg and D. Wallace, (eds) *Changes in Working Life* (London: Wiley).

Bower, T.G.R. (1965) 'Stimulus variables determining space perception in infants', *Science*, 149, pp. 88–9.

British Psychological Society (1978) *Ethical Principles for Research on Human Subjects* (Leicester: The British Psychological Society).

British Psychological Society (1985) 'A code of conduct for psychologists', *Bulletin of the B.P.S.*, vol. 38, pp. 41–3.

British Psychological Society (1986) *How about Psychology: A guide to courses and careers* (Leicester: BPS Books).

British Psychological Society (1988) *Career Choices in Psychology* (Leicester: BPS Books).

British Psychological Society (1989a) *BPS Careers Pack* (Leicester: BPS Books).

British Psychological Society (1989b) *Putting Psychology to Work* (Leicester: BPS Books).

British Psychological Society (1990) *Ethical Principles for Conducting*

Research with Human Participants (Leicester: The British Psychological Society).

Broadbent, D.E. (1958) *Perception and Communication* (Oxford: Pergamon).

Broadbent, D.E. (1961) *Behaviour* (London: Eyre & Spottiswoode).

Brown, G:D.A. (1990) 'Cognitive science and its relation to psychology', *The Psychologist*, August, pp. 339–43.

Bruner, J.S. (1976) 'Psychology and the Image of Man', *Times Literary Supplement*, 17 Dec.

Cannon, W.B. (1927) 'The James–Lange theory of emotions: a critical examination of an alternative theory', *American Journal of Psychology*, 39, pp. 106–24.

Chapman, A.J. and A. Gale (1982) *Psychology and People: a Tutorial Text* (BPS/Macmillan).

Clegg, F. (1982) *Simple Statistics – A Course Book for the Social Sciences* (Cambridge: Cambridge University Press).

Cohen, G. (1977) *The Psychology of Cognition* (London: Academic Press).

Coile, C. and N.E. Miller (1984) 'How radical animal activists try to mislead humane people', *American Psychologist*, 39, pp. 700–1.

Conover, M.R. (1982) 'Modernizing the scarecrow to protect crops from birds', *Frontiers of Plant Science*, 35, pp. 7–8.

Corsaro, W.A. (1985) *Friendship and Peer Culture in the Early Years* (Norwood, NJ: Ablex Publishing).

Coolican, H. (1990) *Research Methods and Statistics in Psychology* (London: Hodder & Stoughton).

Craik, F. and R. Lockhart (1972) 'Levels of processing', *Journal of Learning and Verbal Behaviour*, 11, pp. 671–84.

Cumming, E. and W. Henry (1961) *Growing Old: a Process of Disengagement* (New York: Basic Books).

Darwin, C. (1872) *The Expression of Emotions in Man and Animals* (London: John Murray: reprinted Chicago: University of Chicago Press).

Dawkins, R. (1976) *The Selfish Gene* (London: Oxford University Press).

De Fries J.C. (1964) 'Effects of prenatal maternal stress on behaviour in mice: A genotype-environment interaction' (Abst.) *Genetics*, 50, 244.

Deutsch, J.A. and D. Deutsch (1963) 'Attention: some theoretical considerations', *Psychological Review*, 70, pp. 80–90.

Department of Education and Science (1982) *Aspects of Secondary Education in England: a survey by HM Inspectors of Schools* (London: HMSO).

Dukes, W.F. (1965) 'N = 1', *Psychological Bulletin*, vol. 64, no. 1, pp. 74–9.)

Ekman, P. (1985) *Telling Lies* (New York: Lyle Stuart).

Ekman, P., R.W. Levenson and W.V. Frieson (1983) 'Autonomic nervous system activity distinguishes among emotions', *Science*, 221, pp. 1208–10.

Ellis, A. (1962) *Reason and Emotion in Psychotherapy* (New York: Lyle Stuart).

Eron, L.D., L.R. Huesmann, M.M. Lefkowitz and L.O. Walder (1972) 'Does television violence cause aggression?', *American Psychologist*, 27, pp. 253–62.

Experimental Psychology Society (1986) *The Use of Animals for Research by Psychologists* (Experimental Psychology Society).

Eysenck, H.J. (1952) 'The effects of psychotherapy: an evaluation', *Journal of Consulting Psychology*, 16, pp. 319–24.

Eysenck, H.J. (1966) 'Personality and experimental psychology', *Bulletin of the British Psychological Society*, 19, (62) pp. 1–28.

Eysenck, H.J. and S.B.G. Eysenck (1964) *Manual of the Eysenck Personality Inventory* (London: University of London Press).

Eysenck, H.J. and G.D. Wilson (1973) *The Experimental Study of Freudian Theories* (London: Methuen).

Fairbairn, S. and G. Fairbairn (eds) (1987) *Psychology, Ethics and Change* (London: Routledge & Kegan Paul).

Falk, J.L. (1956) 'Issues distinguishing idiographic from nomothetic approaches to personality theory', *Psychological Review*, vol. 63, no. 1, pp. 53–62.

Festinger, L., H.W. Riecken and S. Schachter (1956) *When Prophecy Fails* (Minnesota: University of Minnesota Press).

Festinger, L. and J.J. Carlsmith (1959) 'Cognitive consequences of forced compliance', *Journal of Abnormal and Social Psychology*, 58, pp. 293–310.

Freud, A. (1936) *The Ego and the Mechanisms of Defence* (London: Chatto & Windus).

Gallup, G.G. and S.D. Suarez (1985) 'Animal research versus the care and maintenance of pets: the names have been changed but the results remain the same', *American Psychologist*, vol. 40, p. 968.

Gardner, A.R. and B. Gardner. 'Teaching sign language to a chimpanzee', *Science*, 165, pp. 664–72.

Gray, J.A. (1987) 'The ethics and politics of animal experimentation', in H. Beloff and A.M. Colman (eds), *Psychological Survey No.6* (Leicester: The British Psychological Society).

Green, S. (1980) 'Physiological Studies I and II', in J. Radford and E. Govier (eds), *A Textbook of Psychology* (London: Sheldon Press).

Gregory, R.L. (1972) 'Visual Illusions', in B.M. Foss (ed.), *New Horizons in Psychology 1* (Harmondsworth: Penguin).

Gregory, R.L. and J.G. Wallace (1963) 'Recovery from early blindness: a case study', *Experimental Psychological and Social Monograms*, 2.

Gross, R.D. (1987) *Psychology: the Science of Mind and Behaviour* (London: Arnold).

Grossman, S.P. (1960) 'Eating or drinking elicited by direct adenergic or cholinergic stimulation of the hypothalamus', *Science*, 132, pp. 301–2.

Guilford, J.P. (1950) 'Creativity', *American Psychologist*, 5, pp. 444–54.

Hargreaves, D.H. (1967) *Social Relations in a Secondary School* (London: Routledge & Kegan Paul).

Hartmann, E.L. (1973) *The Functions of Sleep* (New Haven, Conn.: Yale University Press).

Hawks, D. (1981) 'The dilemma of clinical practice – Surviving as a clinical psychologist', in McPherson, J.M. and M. Sutton (eds), *Reconstructing Psychological Practice* (London: Croom Helm).

Heather, N. (1976) *Radical Perspectives in Psychology* (London: Methuen).

Hebb, D.O. (1949) *The Organisation of Behavior* (New York: Wiley).

Hebb, D.O. (1974) 'What psychology is about', *The American Psychologist*, 29, pp. 71–87.

Hediger, H. (1951) *Wild Animals in Captivity* (London: Butterworth).

Heidbreder, E. *Seven Psychologies* (Englewood Cliffs, NJ: Prentice-Hall, 1963).

Hess, E.H. (1959) 'Imprinting', *Science*, 130, pp. 133–41.

Hess, E.H. (1972) 'Imprinting in a Natural Laboratory', *Scientific American* 227, pp. 24–31.

Hetherington, E.M. and N.P. Wray (1964) 'Aggression, need for social approval and humour preferences', *Journal of Abnormal and Social Psychology*, 68, pp. 685–9.

Hill, C.J., Z. Rubin and L.A. Peplau (1976) 'Break-ups before marriage: the end of 103 affairs', *Journal of Social Issues*, 32(1), pp. 147–88.

Holt, R. (1962) 'Individuality and generalisation in the psychology or personality', *Journal of Personality*, 30, pp. 377–404.

Hubel, D.H. and T.N. Wiesel (1962) 'Receptive fields in the striate cortex of young visually inexperienced kittens', *Journal of Neurophysiology*, 26, p. 994.

Hull, C.L. (1943) *Principles of Behaviour* (New York: Appleton Century Crofts).

Humphreys, L. (1970) *Tea Room Trade: Impersonal sex in public places* (Chicago: Aldine-Atherton).

Isaacs, W., J. Thomas and I. Goldiamond (1960) 'Applications of operant conditioning to reinstate verbal behaviour in psychotics', *Journal of Speech and Hearing Disorders*, vol. 25, pp. 8–12.

James, W. (1884) 'What is an emotion?', *Mind*, 9, pp. 188–205.

James, W. (1890) *Principles of Psychology* (New York: Holt).

Jouvet, M. (1967) 'Mechanisms of the states of sleep: a neuropharmacological approach', *Research Publications of the Association for Research into Nervous and Mental Disease*, 45, pp. 86–126.

Joy, L.A., M. Kimball and M.L. Zabrack (1977) 'Television exposure and children's aggressive behavior', in T.M. Williams (Chair) 'The impact of television: a natural experiment involving three communities.' Symposium presented at the annual meeting of the Canadian Psychological Association, Vancouver.

Klein, M. (1959) 'Our adult world and its roots in infancy', *Human Relations*, 12, 4, pp. 291–303.

Kline, P. (1984) *Psychology and Freudian Theory: an Introduction* (London: Methuen).

Koestler, A. (1970) *The Ghost in the Machine* (London: Pan Books).

Kohlberg, L. (1975) 'The cognitive–developmental approach to moral education', Phi Delta Kappan, June, pp. 670–7.

Koriat, A., R. Melkman, J.R. Averill and R.S. Lazarus (1972) 'Self-control of emotional reactions to a stressful film', *Journal of Personality*, 40, pp. 601–19.

Krebs, J.R., A. Kacelnik and P. Taylor (1978) 'Optimal sampling by birds; an experiment with great tits (Parus major)', *Nature*, 275, pp. 27–31.

Kuhn, T.S. (1962) *The Structure of Scientific Revolutions* (Chicago: University of Chicago Press).

Lamiell, J.T. (1981) 'Toward an idiothetic psychology of personality', *American Psychologist*, vol. 36, no. 3, pp. 276–89.

Lang, P.J. and B.G. Melamed (1969) 'Case report: avoidance conditioning therapy of an infant with chronic ruminative vomiting', *Journal of Abnormal Psychology*, 74, pp. 1–8.

Lashley, K.S. (1929) *Brain mechanisms and Intelligence* (Chicago, Illinois: University of Chicago Press).

Lange, C.J. (1967) *The Emotions* (translation of Lange's 1885 monograph) in C.J. Lange and W. James (eds) *The Emotions* (New York: Haffner Publishing Co). (Facsimile of 1922 edition.)

Lazarus, R.S. (1971) *Personality*, 2nd edn (Englewood Cliffs, NJ: Prentice-Hall).

Lazarus, R.S. (1974) 'Cognitive and coping processes in emotion', in B. Weiner (ed.), *Cognitive Views of Human Motivation* (New York: Academic Press).

Lea, S.E.G. (1984) *Instinct, Environment and Behaviour* (London: Methuen).

Legge, D. (1975) *An Introduction to Psychological Science* (London: Methuen).

Lerner, R.M. (1986) *Concepts and Theories of Human Development*, 2nd edn (New York: Random House).

Leyhausen, P. (1973) 'On the function and relative hierarchy of moods', in K. Lorenz and P. Leyhausen (eds), *Motivation of Human and Animal Behavior* (New York: Van Nostrand).

Lilly, J.C. (1977) *The Deep Self* (New York: Simon & Schuster).

Loftus, E.F. (1979) *Eyewitness Testimony* (Cambridge, Mass.: Harvard University Press).

Lorenz, K. (1937), in W. Sluckin (1972), *Imprinting and Early Learning* (London: Methuen).

Lorenz, K. (1966) *On Aggression* (London: Methuen).

Lovaas, O.I. (1973) *Behavioral Treatment of Autistic Children* (Morristown, NJ: General Learning Press).

Luce, G.G. (1971) *Body Time: Physiological Rhythms and Social Stress* (New York: Pantheon).

Malim, T. and A. Birch (1989) *Social Psychology* (London: Macmillan).

Maslow, A.H. (1959) 'Cognition of being in the peak experences', *Journal of Genetic Psychology*, 94, pp. 43–66.

Maslow, A.H. (1968) *Towards a Psychology of Being* (New York: Van Nostrand).

Maslow, A.H. (1971) *The Farther Reaches of Human Nature* (New York: Viking).

Masters, R.E.L. and J. Houston (1966) *Varieties of Psychedelic Experience* (New York: Holt, Rinehart & Winston).

Masters, W.H. and V.E. Johnson (1966) *Human Sexual Response* (Boston, Mass.: Little, Brown).

McClelland, D.C., J.W. Atkinson, R.A. Clark and E.L. Lowell (1953) *The Achievement Motive* (New York: Appleton Century Crofts).

Medcof, J. and J. Roth (eds) (1979) *Approaches to Psychology* (Milton Keynes, OU Press).

Milgram, S. (1974) *Obedience to Authority* (New York: Harper & Row).

Miller, N.E. (1985) 'The Value of Behavioral Research on Animals', *American Psychologist*, 40, pp. 423–40.

Miller, S. (1975) *Experimental Design and Statistics* (London: Methuen).

Miron, N. (1968) 'Issues and implications of operant conditioning; the primary ethical consideration', *Hospital and Community Psychiatry*, 19, pp. 226–8.

Morris, D. (1978) *Manwatching* (St Albans, Herts: Triad/Panther).

Morris, J.B. and A.T. Beck (1974) 'The efficacy of anti-depressant drugs: a review of research (1958–72)', *Archives of General Psychiatry*, 30, pp. 667–74.

Mowrer, O.H. and W.A. Mowrer (1938) 'Enuresis: a method for its study and treatment', *American Journal of Orthopsychiatry*, 8, pp. 436–47.

Neisser, U. (1964) 'Visual Search', *Scientific American*, 210, pp. 94–101.

Neugarten, B.L. (1973) 'Personality change in late life: a developmental perspective', in C. Eisdorfer and M.P. Lawton (eds), *Psychology of Adult Development and Aging* (Washington DC.: American Psychological Association).

Neugarten, B.L. (1977) 'Personality in aging', in J.E. Birren and K.W. Schaie (eds), *Handbook of the Psychology of Aging* (New York: Van Nostrand).

Newell, A., J.C. Shaw and H.A. Simon (1958) 'Elements of a theory of human problem solving', *Psychological Review*, 65, pp. 151–66.

Newell, A. and H.A. Simon (1972) *Human Problem Solving* (Englewood Cliffs, NJ: Prentice-Hall).

Norman, D.A. (1976) *Memory and Attention: an Introduction to Human Information Processing*, 2nd edn (New York: Wiley).

Norman, D.A. and D.G. Bobrow (1976) 'On the analysis of performance operating characteristics', *Psychological Review*, 83, pp. 508–10.

Olds, J. and P. Milner (1954) 'Positive reinforcement produced by electrical stimulation of septal area and other regions of rat brain', *Journal of Comparative Physiological Psychology*, 47, pp. 419–27.

Ora, J.P. (1965) 'Characteristics of the volunteer for psychological investigations', *Office of Naval Research Contract 2149* (03), Technical Report 27.

Orne, M.T. (1962) 'On the social psychology of the psychological experiment: with particular reference to demand characteristics and their implications', *American Psychologist*, 17, pp. 776–83.

Onhe, M.T. and Evans F.J (1965) 'Social control in the psychological experiment: anti-social behaviour and hypnosis'. *Journal of Personality and Social Psychology*, 51, pp. 189–200.

Pavlov I. (1927) (trans. G.V. Anrep) *Conditioned Reflexes* (London: Oxford University Press).

Peele, S. (1981) 'Reductionism in the psychology of the eighties: Can biochemistry eliminate addiction, mental illness, and pain?', *American Psychologist*, vol. 36, no. 8, pp. 807–18.

Peirce, C.S. (1951) 'The Fixation of Belief', in M.H. Fisch (ed.), *Classic American Philosophers* (New York: Appleton Century Crofts).

Penfield, W. (1975) *The Mystery of the Mind* (Princeton, NJ: Princeton University Press).

Penfield, W. and T. Rasmussen (1957) *The Cerebral Cortex of Man* (New York: Macmillan).

Pervin, L.A. (1984) *Current Controversies and Issues in Personality*, 2nd edn (New York: Wiley).

Pfaffenberger, C. (1963) *The New Knowledge of Dog Behavior* (New York: Howell Book House).

Piaget, J. (1953) *The Origin of Intelligence in the Child* (London: Routledge & Kegan Paul).

Popper, K. (1972) *Conjectures and Refutations: the Growth of Scientific Knowledge*, 4th edn (London: Routledge & Kegan Paul).

Prechtl, H.F.R. and D.J. Beintema (1964) 'The neurological examination of the full term new born infant' in *Clinics in Developmental Meicine* (London: Heinemann).

Putnam, H. (1973) 'Reductionism and the nature of psychology', *Cognition*, 2(1) pp. 131–46.

Raaheim K. and J. Radford (1984) *Your Introduction to Psychology* (Oslo: J.W. Cappelens Forlag a.s.; London: Sigma).

Radford, J. and R. Kirby (1975) *The Person in Psychology* (London: Methuen).

Robertson, I. and Downs S. (1979) 'Learning and the prediction of performance development of trainability testing in the United Kingdom', *Journal of Applied Psychology*, 64, pp. 42–50.

Riegal, K (1976) 'The dialectics of human development', *American Psychologist*, 31, pp. 689–99.

Robins, L.N., D.H. Davis and D.W. Goodwin (1974) 'Drug use by the army enlisted men in Vietnam: a follow-up on their return home', *American Journal of Epidemiology*, 99, pp. 235–49.

Robson, C. (1984) *Experiment Design and Statistics in Psychology*, 2nd edn (Harmondsworth: Penguin).

Roediger, H.L. Rushton, J.P. Capaldi, E.D. and Paris, S.G. (1987) *Psychology*, 2nd edn (Boston/Toronto: Little-Brown).

Rogers, C.R. (1951) *Client-centred Therapy* (Boston, Mass.: Houghton Mifflin).

Rogers, C.R. (1961) *On Becoming a Person* (Boston, Mass.: Houghton Mifflin) (reprinted 1967).

Rolls, E.T. (1979) 'Effects of electrical stimulation of the brain on behavior', *Psychology Surveys*, 2, pp. 191–269.

Rose, S. (1976) The Conscious Brain (Harmondsworth: Penguin).

Rosenthal, R. (1966) *Experimenter Effects in Behavioral Research* (New York: Appleton Century Crofts).

Rosenthal, R. (1969) 'Interpersonal Expectations: Effects of Experimenter's Hypothesis', in R. Rosenthal and R.L. Rosnow (eds), *Artefacts in Behavioral Research* (New York: Academic Press).

Rushton, J.P. (1978) 'Urban density and altruism, helping strangers in a Canadian city, suburb and small town'. *Psychological Reports*, 33, pp. 987–90.

Rutter, M., B. Maughan, P. Mortimore and J. Ouston (1979) *Fifteen Thousand Hours* (London: Open Books).

Schachter, S. and J.E. Singer (1962) 'Cognitive, social and physiological determinants of an emotional state', *Psychological Review*, 69, pp. 379–99.

Schaffer, R. (1977) *Mothering* (London: Fontana).

Schulz, D. (1987) *A History of Modern Psychology*, 4th edn (New York: Academic Press).

Seligman, M.E. (1974) 'Depression and Learned Helplessness', in R.J Freedom and M.M Katz (eds), *The Psychology of Depression* (Washington DC: V.H. Winston).

Selye, H. (1956) *The Stress of Life* (New York: McGraw-Hill).

Selye, H. (1974) *Stress Without Distress* (Philadelphia: Lippincott).

Shallice, T. and E.K. Warrington, (1977) 'Auditory-verbal short-term memory impairment and conduction aphasia', *Brain and Language*, 4, pp. 479–91.

Shayer, M. and H. Wylam (1978) 'The distribution of Piagetian stages of thinking in British middle and secondary school children II: 14–16-year-olds and sex differentials', *British Journal of Educational Psychology*, 48, pp. 62–70.

Sherrington, R., J. Bryjolfsson and collaborators (1988) 'Localisation of a susceptibility locus for schizophrenia on chromosome 5', *Nature*, 336, pp. 164–7.

Shostrum, E.L., R.R. Knapp and L. Knapp (1976) 'Validation of the personal orientation dimensions. An inventory for the dimensions of actualising', *Educational and Psychological Measurement*, vol. 36(2) pp. 491–4.

Simmons, J.V. Jnr. (1981) 'Project sea hunt: a report on prototype development and tests', *Technical Report No. 746* (San Diego, CA: Naval Ocean System Center).

Skinner, B.F. (1938) *The Behavior of Organisms* (New York: Appleton–Century–Croft).

Skinner, B.F. (1948) *Walden Two* (New York: Macmillan).

Skinner, B.F. (1953) *Science and Human Behavior* (New York: Macmillan).

Skinner, B.F. (1971) *Beyond Freedom and Dignity* (London: Jonathan Cape).

Solomon, R.L. and J.D. Corbit (1974) 'An opponent-process theory of motivation: Pt. 1. Temporal dynamics of affect', *Psychological Review*, 81, pp. 119–45.

Sperling, G. (1960) 'The information available in brief visual presentation', in *Psychological Monographs*, 74, no. 498.

Sternbach, R.A. (1962) 'Assessing differential autonomic patterns in emotions', *Journal of Psychosomatic Research*, 6, pp. 87–91.

Stoner, J.A.F. (1961) 'A comparison of individual and group decisions involving risk', *unpublished Master's thesis, Sloan School of Management*, Cambridge Mass., MIT.

Sylva, K.D., C. Roy and M. Painter (1980) *Childwatching at Playgroup and Nursery School* (London: Grant McIntyre).

Tedeschi, J.T., S. Lindskold and P. Rosenfeld (1985) *Introduction to Social Psychology* (New York: West).

Tesch, S.A. (1983) 'Review of friendship development across the life-span', *Human Development*, 26, pp. 266–76.

Teska, P.T. (1947) 'The mentality of hydrocephalics and a description of an interesting case', *Journal of Psychology*, 23, pp. 197–203.

Thoday, J.M. (1965) in J.M. Meade and A.S. Parkes (eds), *Biological Aspects of Social Problems* (London: Oliver and Boyd).

Tinbergen, N. and E.C. Perdeck (1950) 'On the stimulus situation releasing the begging response in the newly hatched herring gull chick', *Behaviour*, 3, pp. 1–39.

Treisman, A. (1964a) 'Verbal cues, language and meaning in selective attention', *American Journal of Psychology*, 77, pp. 206–19.

Treisman, A. (1964b) 'Monitoring and storing of irrelevant messages in selective attention', *Journal of Verbal Learning and Verbal Behaviour*, 3, pp. 449–59.

Valentine, E.R. (1982) *Conceptual Issues in Psychology* (London: George Allen & Unwin).

Valins, S. (1966) 'Cognitive effects of false heart-rate feedback', *Journal of Personality and Social Psychology*, 4, pp. 400–8.

Vernon, P.E. (1969) *Intelligence and Cultural Environment* (London: Methuen).

Wadeley, A. (1991), *Ethics in Psychological Research and Practice* (Leicester: The British Psychological Society).

Walker, S. (1984) *Learning Theory and Behaviour Modification* (London: Methuen).

Wallach, M.A. and L. Wallach (1983) *Psychology's Sanction for Selfishness* (San Francisco: Freeman).

Warr, P.B. (ed.) (1978) *Psychology at Work* (Harmondsworth: Penguin).

Watson, J.B. (1913) 'Psychology as the behaviourist views it', *Psychological Review* 20, pp. 158–77.

Watson J.B. (1919) *Psychology from the Standpoint of the Behaviourist* (Philadelphia: Lippincott).

Watson, J.B. and R. Rayner (1920) 'Conditioned emotional reactions', *Journal of Experimental Psychology*, 3, pp. 1–4.

Weber, S.J. and T.D. Cook (1972) 'Subject effects in laboratory research: An examination of subject roles, demand characteristics and valid inference', *Psychological Bulletin*, 77, pp. 273–95.

Wertheimer, M. (1972) *Fundamental Issues in Psychology* (New York: Holt Rinehart & Winston).

Westland, G. (1978) *Current Crises in Psychology* (London: Heinmann).

Whyte, W.F. (1955) *Street Corner Society: the social structure of an Italian slum* (Chicago: Chicago University Press).

Wilson, E.O. (1975) *Sociobiology* (Cambridge, Mass.: Havard University Press).

Windelband, W. (1904) *Geschichte und Naturwissenschaft*, 3rd edn (Strasburg: Heitz).

Witkin, H.A., D.R. Goodenough, S.A. Karp, R.B. Dyke and H.F. Faterson (1962) *Psychological Differentiation* (New York: Wiley).

Woodworth, R.S. and Sheehan, M.R. (1965) *Contemporary Schools of Psychology* (London: Methuen).

Wundt, W. (1879) *An Introduction to Psychology* (trans. R. Pinter) (London: George Allen).

Young, R.F., R.A. Feldman, R. Kroenig, W. Fulton and J. Morris (1984) 'Electrical stimulation of the brain in the treatment of chronic pain in man', in L. Kruger and J.C. Liebeskind (eds), *Advances in Pain Research and Therapy*, vol. 6, pp. 289–303.

Zimbardo, P.G. (1973) 'On the ethics of intervention in human psychological research: with special reference to the Stanford prison experiment', *Cognition*, 2(2) pp. 243–56.

Zimbardo, P.G., C. Haney and W.C. Banks (1973) 'A Pirandellian Prison', *New York Times Sunday Magazine*, 8 April 1973, pp. 38–60.

Zinberg, N. (1974) 'The Search for Rational Approaches to Heroin Use', in P.G. Bourne (ed.) *Addiction* (New York: Academic Press).

Index